张惠芬 ● 编著

张老师教汉字

汉字识写课本 下

英译 · 熊文华

插图 · 丁永寿

READING AND WRITING CHINESE CHARACTERS
ZHANG LAOSHI JIAO HANZI
(B)

北京语言大学出版社
BEIJING LANGUAGE AND CULTURE
UNIVERSITY PRESS

图书在版编目（CIP）数据

张老师教汉字·汉字识写课本（下）/ 张惠芬编著.
—北京：北京语言大学出版社，2005（2016.10 重印）
ISBN 978 – 7 – 5619 – 1464 – 9

Ⅰ．张…
Ⅱ．张…
Ⅲ．汉字 – 对外汉语教学 – 教材
Ⅳ．H195.4

中国版本图书馆 CIP 数据核字（2005）第 071020 号

书　　名：	张老师教汉字·汉字 识写课本（下）
责任印制：	姜正周

出版发行：**北京语言大学出版社**
社　　址：北京市海淀区学院路 15 号　邮政编码 100083
网　　址：www.blcup.com
电　　话：发行部　82303650/3591/3648
　　　　　编辑部　82303647
　　　　　读者服务部　82303653
　　　　　网上订购电话　82303908
　　　　　客户服务信箱　service@blcup.com
印　　刷：北京中科印刷有限公司
经　　销：全国新华书店

版　　次：2005 年 11 月第 1 版　2016 年 10 月第 10 次印刷
开　　本：787 毫米×1092 毫米　1/16　印张：15.75
字　　数：235 千字
书　　号：ISBN 978 – 7 – 5619 – 1464 – 9/H·04016
定　　价：39.00 元

凡有印装质量问题，本社负责调换。电话：82303590

使 用 建 议

　　《张老师教汉字》是为零起点来华留学生、特别是非汉字文化圈的初学者编写的汉字选修课教材。本教材根据来华留学生汉字学习的实际情况,编为《汉字识写课本》和《汉字拼读课本》两种,使写字教学和识字教学适当分流。

　　(1)《汉字识写课本》用"图画法"作为形义联想的生发点,以形声字形旁归类为主线,侧重汉字的书写、字源分析和形体结构分析,旨在帮助学习者清晰构建与汉字相适应的认知结构。

　　(2)《汉字拼读课本》用"拼形法"建立汉字之间的关系联想和类推,以形声字声旁归类为主线,在"记忆窍门"的形式中凸显汉字学习策略,意在给学生一个系统,将构字规律转化为识字规律。

　　(3)为更有效地掌握汉字,本教材还注意字义与词义的关系,给所学汉字提供了一些由该字组成的词,又给每一个应当掌握的词提供了例句,希望在语境中加深对这些字、词的理解。

　　(4)本教材还在汉字教学的同时介绍汉字学习策略,体现再循环汉字记忆法,遇生想熟,寻找相似;以熟带生,扩展类化,在不断复现、推演中掌握尽可能多的汉字。

　　《张老师教汉字》依据国家汉办《汉字水平词汇与汉字等级大纲》,共收录汉字 1885 个,包括全部甲、乙级字以及 260 多个丙、丁级字,另外还有 20 个超纲字,如"翰""韩""酪"等,以补学生所需。《汉字识写课本》收录汉字 780 个,其中甲级字 630 个左右,乙级字 120 多个,以及少量的作为部首的丙、丁级字。

　　《汉字识写课本》共 25 课,《汉字拼读课本》共 30 课,每课均需两课时。

　　《汉字识写课本》配有练习册,《汉字拼读课本》配有 CD。

北京语言大学　张惠芬

Suggestions on How to Use

Learning Chinese Characters from Ms. Zhang is a set of textbooks for an elective course of Chinese characters for foreign students in China without any Chinese learning experience, especially those beginners coming from the non-Chinese character-culture. In consideration of the real situation, in which those foreign students learn Chinese characters in China, this set of textbooks includes *Reading and Writing Chinese Characters and From Characters to Words*, separating in a proper way the teaching of writing Chinese characters from that of reading Chinese characters.

1. With the help of pictures, *Reading and Writing Chinese Characters* encourages learners to associate pictographic elements with meanings. Grouping pictophonetic characters by their pictographic elements, the book lays special emphasis on writing characters and analyzing the origin and structure of the characters, aiming at helping learners establish a cognitive construct for Chinese characters.

2. Highlighting the formation of a character by combining different component parts, *From Characters to Words* establishes association and analogy among Chinese characters. The book groups pictophonetic characters by their phonetic elements and provides various tips for memorizing characters, aiming at helping learners master a system, by which they can change the regular pattern of Chinese characters' formation into a law of learning Chinese characters.

3. To help learners master Chinese characters effectively, the set of textbooks pays attention to the relationship between the meaning of the character and that of the word by offering some words formed by using the character being learned and providing some example sentences for each of the words to be mastered. It is hoped that learners will gain a better understanding of the characters and the words in context.

4. While carrying out Chinese characters teaching, the set of textbooks also introduces various learning strategies, such as memorizing characters by recycling them repeatedly, associating new characters with the familiar ones by finding the similarity between them, and learning new characters with the help of the old ones etc. These strategies will assist learners to master more Chinese characters.

In accordance with HSK Guidelines for Chinese Words and Characters issued by the National Office for Teaching Chinese as a Foreign Language, *Learning Characters from Ms. Zhang* includes 1, 885 Chinese characters altogether, among which are all the Chinese characters of Class A and Class B, over 260 of Class C and Class D characters and 20 not included in the guidelines (such as "翰", "韩" and "酩"). In *Reading and Writing Chinese Characters* 780 Chinese characters are taught, among which about 630 are of Class A characters, over 120 of Class B characters and a few of Class C and Class D characters as radicals.

Reading and Writing Chinese Characters has 25 lessons and *From Characters to Words*, 30. Each of the lessons takes 2 hours to teach.

Reading and Writing Chinese Characters is equipped with a workbook and *From Characters to Words* with CDs.

Zhang Huifen
Beijing Language and Culture University

目　录
CONTENTS

3

13
LESSON

第十三课

 基本知识
Rudiments of Chinese Characters

汉字的偏旁(三)
The Radicals of Chinese Characters (C)

偏旁最初都是独体字。随着汉字的演变,有的独体字做偏旁时,形体上有所变化,它们已不再单独成字使用了。如:

> Originally all radicals were Chinese single-element characters. In the process of the development of the Chinese characters, some of the single-element characters have been used as radicals, whose forms and structures have been modified. They are no longer used independently as characters, for example:

$$人 \rightarrow 亻 : 你 \qquad 竹 \rightarrow 竹 : 等$$
$$示 \rightarrow 礻 : 祝 \qquad 足 \rightarrow 𧾷 : 跑$$
$$衣 \rightarrow 衤 : 被$$

还有些独体字做偏旁时,随着汉字的简化而有较大的形体变化。如:

> As a result of the simplification of the Chinese characters, the forms and structures of some of the single-element characters used as radicals have been greatly modified, for example:

$$言 \rightarrow 言 \rightarrow 讠 : 试$$
$$食 \rightarrow 食 \rightarrow 饣 : 饭$$
$$金 \rightarrow 金 \rightarrow 钅 : 钱$$

1

生字词表
List of New Characters and Words

1.	示	shì	to show
	表示	biǎoshì	to express
2.	祝	zhù	to wish
	祝贺	zhùhè	to congratulate
3.	礼	lǐ	rite
	礼物	lǐwù	gift
	礼拜	lǐbài	week
	礼拜天	lǐbàitiān	Sunday
4.	票	piào	ticket
	车票	chēpiào	bus (train) ticket
	机票	jīpiào	air ticket
	门票	ménpiào	entrance ticket
5.	被	bèi	(a passive particle)，quilt
	被子	bèizi	quilt
6.	衬	chèn	cloth lining
	衬衣	chènyī	shirt
7.	衫	shān	unlined upper garment
	衬衫	chènshān	shirt
8.	裙	qún	skirt
	裙子	qúnzi	skirt
9.	裤	kù	trousers
	裤子	kùzi	trousers
10.	袜	wà	socks
	袜子	wàzi	socks，stockings

11.	笔	bǐ	pen，(a measure word)
	毛笔	máobǐ	writing brush
12.	第	dì	(indicating ordinal numbers)
	第一	dì yī	first
13.	答	dá	to reply
	回答	huídá	to answer
14.	等	děng	to wait
	等车	děng chē	to wait for a bus/train
	等一下	děng yíxià	to wait a while
15.	篮	lán	basket
	篮球	lánqiú	basketball
16.	算	suàn	to count，to plan，to regard as
	打算	dǎsuan	to plan
	计算机	jìsuànjī	computer
	算了	suàn le	to forget it，to let it pass
17.	筷	kuài	chopstick
	筷子	kuàizi	chopsticks
18.	踢	tī	to kick
	踢足球	tī zúqiú	to play football
19.	路	lù	road
	十字路口	shízì lùkǒu	four-ways intersection，crossroad
20.	跟	gēn	to follow
21.	跑	pǎo	to run
	长跑	chángpǎo	long-distance running
22.	饭	fàn	meal
	早饭	zǎofàn	breakfast
	午饭	wǔfàn	lunch
	晚饭	wǎnfàn	supper，dinner
23.	馆	guǎn	hall
	饭馆儿	fànguǎnr	restaurant
	咖啡馆	kāfēiguǎn	café

24. 饮	yǐn	to drink
饮料	yǐnliào	drinks
25. 饿	è	hungry
26. 饱	bǎo	to have eaten one's fill
27. 饺	jiǎo	dumpling
饺子	jiǎozi	dumpling
28. 餐	cān	meal
餐厅	cāntīng	dining hall
快餐	kuàicān	fast-food
中餐	zhōngcān	Chinese food
西餐	xīcān	Western-style food
29. 金	jīn	gold
现金	xiànjīn	cash
30. 铁	tiě	iron
地铁	dìtiě	subway
31. 铅	qiān	lead
铅笔	qiānbǐ	pencil
32. 钢	gāng	steel
钢笔	gāngbǐ	fountain pen
33. 钟	zhōng	clock，bell
……点钟	…diǎnzhōng	o'clock
钟头	zhōngtóu	an hour
34. 银	yín	silver
银行	yínháng	bank
35. 钱	qián	money
钱包	qiánbāo	purse, wallet
36. 锻	duàn	to temper
锻炼	duànliàn	physical training
37. 错	cuò	wrong
不错	búcuò	right，not bad

生字的结构和书写
The Structures and Writing of the New Characters

礻　　示字旁　shì zì páng　The Radical of 礻

礻	礻	礻	礻								

　　"礻"是由"示"演变而来的,"示"做形旁的字多与祭祀、鬼神等有关,示字旁常在字的左侧,写做"礻",有时亦可在字的下部,写做"示"。

The characters with the pictophonetic radical 礻 derived from the pictographic character 示 are often associated with worshipping, sacrifices, gods or ghosts. When standing on the left of a character it is written as 礻. When used at the lower part of a character it is written as 示.

1 示　shì　to show

表示　biǎoshì　to express

古字像由一横一竖两石块搭成的祭祀鬼神的供桌。

The ancient written form of 示 is in the shape of a two-stone altar for worshipping.

示	示	示	示	示						

上横短,下横长。下面是"小"。

There are two horizontals of which the top one is shorter. Underneath is a 小.

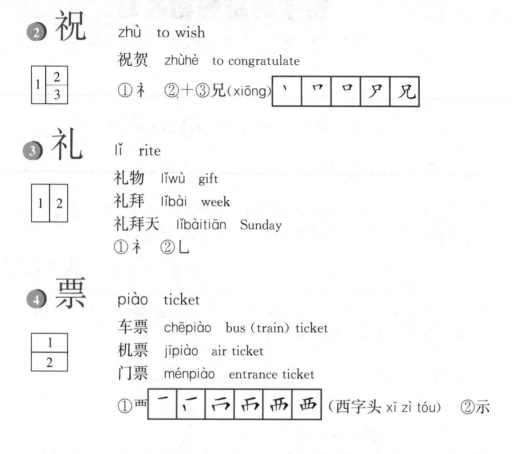

2 祝 zhù to wish

祝贺 zhùhè to congratulate

①礻 ②＋③兄(xiōng) 丶 丷 口 尸 兄

3 礼 lǐ rite

礼物 lǐwù gift

礼拜 lǐbài week

礼拜天 lǐbàitiān Sunday

①礻 ②乚

4 票 piào ticket

车票 chēpiào bus (train) ticket

机票 jīpiào air ticket

门票 ménpiào entrance ticket

①覀 一 厂 冖 襾 西 西 (西字头 xī zì tóu) ②示

礻 衣字旁 yī zì páng The Radical of 礻

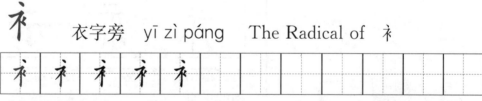

"礻"是由"衣"演变而来的,象形字"衣"见上册第107页,"礻"做形旁的字多与衣服有关。衣字旁常在字的左侧,写做"礻",有时也可在字的下边,写做"衣"。

The characters with the pictophonetic radical 礻 (see page 107, Textbook I) derived from the pictographic character 衣 are often related to clothing. When standing on the left of a character, it is written as 礻. Sometimes it is also used at the lower part of a character.

5 被

bèi （a passive particle），quilt

被子　bèizi　quilt

1	2

①衤　②皮 | 一 | 厂 | 广 | 皮 | 皮 |

6 衬

chèn　cloth lining

衬衣　chènyī　shirt

1	2

①衤　②寸

7 衫

shān　unlined upper garment

衬衫　chènshān　shirt

1	2

①衤　②彡 | ノ | ク | 彡 |

8 裙

qún　skirt

裙子　qúnzi　skirt

1	2

①衤　②君(jūn) | 刁 | 刁 | 刁 | 尹 | 君 |

9 裤

kù　trousers

裤子　kùzi　trousers

1	2

①衤　②库(kù) | 广 | 库 |

10 袜

wà　socks

袜子　wàzi　socks，stockings

1	2

①衤　②末

⺮

竹字头　zhú zì tóu　The Radical of ⺮

⺮	⺮	⺮	⺮	⺮	⺮						

"⺮"是由"竹"演变而来的,象形字"竹"见上册第81页。"⺮"做形旁的字常与竹子有关。竹字头在字的上部。

The characters with the pictophonetic radical ⺮ derived from the pictographic character 竹 (see page 81, Textbook I) are often related to bamboo. It is used on the top of a character.

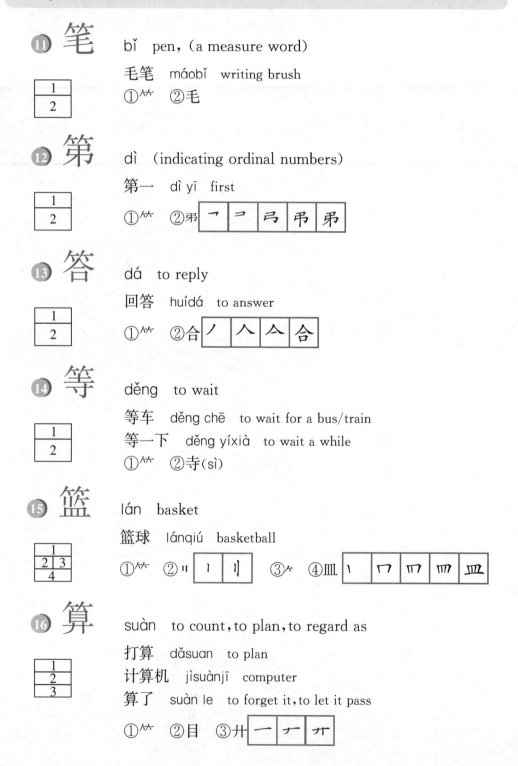

⑪ 笔　bǐ　pen，(a measure word)

1
2

毛笔　máobǐ　writing brush
①⺮　②毛

⑫ 第　dì　(indicating ordinal numbers)

1
2

第一　dì yī　first
①⺮　②弔 | ⺈ | ⺬ | 弓 | 弔 | 弟 |

⑬ 答　dá　to reply

1
2

回答　huídá　to answer
①⺮　②合 | ノ | 八 | 人 | 合 |

⑭ 等　děng　to wait

1
2

等车　děng chē　to wait for a bus/train
等一下　děng yíxià　to wait a while
①⺮　②寺(sì)

⑮ 篮　lán　basket

1	
2	3
4	

篮球　lánqiú　basketball
①⺮　②⺆ | 丨 | 刂 |　③⺊　④皿 | 丨 | 冂 | 皿 | 皿 | 皿 |

⑯ 算　suàn　to count, to plan, to regard as

1
2
3

打算　dǎsuan　to plan
计算机　jìsuànjī　computer
算了　suàn le　to forget it, to let it pass
①⺮　②目　③卅 | 一 | 艹 | 卅 |

17 筷　kuài　chopstick

筷子　kuàizi　chopsticks

1	
2	3

①⺮　②+③快

丶	丷	忄	忄	忄	快	快

足　足字旁　zú zì páng　The Radical of ⻊

⻊	⻊	⻊	⻊	⻊	⻊	⻊			

"⻊"是由"足"演化而来的,象形字"足"见上册第 64 页。"足"做形旁的字多与脚的活动有关,足字旁一般在字的左侧,写做"⻊",最后两笔撇、捺改为竖和提。

The characters with the pictophonetic radical ⻊ derived from the pictographic character 足 (see page 64, Textbook I) are often related to the movement of feet. When standing on the left it is written as ⻊ with its left and right fallings replaced by a vertical and a rising stroke, respectively.

18 踢　tī　to kick

踢足球　tī zúqiú　to play football

1	2

①⻊　②易

19 路　lù　road

十字路口　shízì lùkǒu　four-ways intersection, crossroad

1	2
	3

①⻊　②+③各(gè)

丿	夂	夂	各

20 跟　gēn　to follow

1	2

①⻊　②艮(gěn)

乛	彐	彐	艮	艮	艮

21 跑　pǎo　to run

长跑　chángpǎo　long-distance running

1	2
	3

①⻊　②+③包(bāo)

丿	勹	勺	匀	包

饣　食字旁　shí zì páng　The Radical of 饣

饣	饣	饣								

"饣"是由"食"演变而来的。象形字"食"见上册第 94 页。"食"做形旁的字多与饮食有关,食字旁常在字的左侧,写做"饣"。有时亦可在字的下边,写做"食"。

The characters with the pictophonetic radical 饣 derived from the pictographic character 食（see page 94, Textbook I）are often connected with food and drink. When standing on the left of a character it is written as 饣. Sometimes it is used at the lower part of a character.

㉒ 饭 fàn　meal

早饭　zǎofàn　breakfast
午饭　wǔfàn　lunch
晚饭　wǎnfàn　supper, dinner
①饣　②反(fǎn)

一	厂	厉	反

㉓ 馆 guǎn　hall

饭馆儿　fànguǎnr　restaurant
咖啡馆　kāfēiguǎn　café
①饣　②+③官(guān)

丶	丷	宀	宀	宁	宁	官	官

㉔ 饮 yǐn　to drink

饮料　yǐnliào　drinks
①饣　②欠(qiàn)

丿	亇	夕	欠

㉕ 饿 è　hungry

①饣　②我

㉖ 饱 bǎo　to have eaten one's fill

①饣　②包

27 饺   jiǎo   dumpling

饺子   jiǎozi   dumpling

1	2

①饣   ②交

28 餐   cān   meal

1	2
3	

餐厅   cāntīng   dining hall
快餐   kuàicān   fast-food
中餐   zhōngcān   Chinese food
西餐   xīcān   Western-style food

①歺 | 丶 | ⺊ | ⺊ | 歺 | 歺 | ②又   ③食

⻐   金字旁   jīn zì páng   The Radical of ⻐

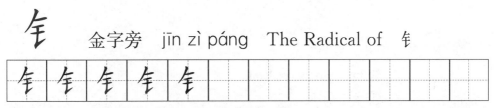

"⻐"是由"金"演变而来的。"金"做形旁的字一般与金属及金属制品有关。金字旁在字的左侧写成"⻐"。

The characters with the pictophonetic radical ⻐ derived from the pictographic character 金 are often connected with metals or their products. When used on the left it is written as ⻐.

29 金   jīn   gold

1	
2	

现金   xiànjīn   cash

①人   ②壬 | 一 | 二 | 千 | 千 | 壬 | 壬 |

30 铁   tiě   iron

1	2

地铁   dìtiě   subway

①⻐   ②失(shī) | 丿 | 丶 | ⺧ | 失 | 失 |

31 铅　qiān　lead

铅笔　qiānbǐ　pencil
①钅　②几　③口

1	2
	3

32 钢　gāng　steel

钢笔　gāngbǐ　fountain pen
①钅　②冈(gāng)

1	2

33 钟　zhōng　clock, bell

……点钟　…diǎnzhōng　o'clock

钟头　zhōngtóu　an hour
①钅　②中

1	2

34 银　yín　silver

银行　yínháng　bank
①钅　②艮

1	2

35 钱　qián　money

钱包　qiánbāo　purse, wallet
①钅　②戋(jiān)　一　二　𡈼　戋　戋

1	2

36 锻　duàn　to temper

锻炼　duànliàn　physical training
①钅
②+③+④段(duàn)　ノ　ｒ　ｆ　ｆ　钅　卧　段　段

1	2	3
		4

37 错　cuò　wrong

不错　búcuò　right, not bad
①钅　②艹　③日

1	2
	3

认读词、词组和句子

Read the Following Words，Phrases and Sentences

一、认读词、词组

Read the Following Words and Phrases.

票：车票　机票　火车票　月票　球票　门票　发票
　　售票员

笔：钢笔　铅笔　毛笔　一支笔　亲笔　笔头作业

等：等车　等人　等一等　等飞机　等火车　等一下

算：打算　计算机　算了　算一算

路：马路　路口　十字路口　一条路　路上　路灯
　　公路　378路公共汽车

饭：吃饭　早饭　午饭　晚饭　米饭

馆：饭馆儿　咖啡馆　饺子馆　酒馆
　　茶(chá)馆(teahouse)

餐：餐厅　中餐　西餐　快餐　早餐　午餐　晚餐
　　一餐饭

金：金钱　金币　金笔　金块　金条　美金　租金
　　奖(jiǎng)学金(scholarship)

篮：篮球　篮子

跑：跑步　长跑

铁：铁路　地铁　铁门　铁块

钟：三点钟　一个钟头　钟楼

钱：有钱　没钱　多少钱　钱包　一块钱
　　一万三千四百五十块钱

二、认读下列句子
Read the Following Sentences.

1. 下礼拜去广州的飞机票买好了吗?

2. 银行东边的咖啡馆上午九点才开门。

3. 学生餐厅的人太多了,我们去学校西边的那个饭馆儿
   吃饭吧。

4. 金成汉每天早上七点钟去足球场跑步,下午四点以后
   跟朋友们一起打篮球、踢足球。

5. 今天是你的生日,我买了这件礼物向你表示祝贺。

6. 被子、衬衫、裙子、裤子和袜子在衣柜里,鞋子在桌子
   下面。

7. 你能不能用筷子吃饭?

8. 这种钢笔、铅笔多少钱一支? 那种毛笔呢?

9. 他今天是坐地铁来学校的,没有坐出租车。

10. 我刚才太饿了,吃了二十个饺子,还喝了不少饮料,现
    在又太饱了。

11. 这是我第一次来中国。

12. 他打算明年去北京大学学习计算机专业。

13. 那个十字路口的北边有一个西餐馆,牛肉做得不错。

14. 我身上的现金不多,一共才两百多块钱。

15. 我在这儿等了他半个钟头了,他还没来。算了,不
    等了。

第十四课

基本知识
Rudiments of Chinese Characters

汉字形体的结构方式
The Structure of Chinese Characters

　　汉字的字形结构可以分为独体字和合体字两大类。独体字是指由笔画组成的、不能再分成两部分的字。其结构图形为☐。如：八、千、女等。

> In terms of the structure Chinese characters may be divided into two types：single characters and combined characters. Single characters, such as 八，千 and 女，are formed by no components but strokes.

　　合体字是指由两个或两个以上的部分组成的字。如：你、好等。从形体构造上来说，构成合体字的部分，有的就是一个独体字，有的是由独体字演变而来的偏旁。所以，独体字是学习汉字的基础。掌握了独体字，合体字的理解和书写就会容易得多。

> Combined characters such as 你 and 好 etc. contain two or more parts. Some of the components of the combined characters are single characters by themselves, or radicals derived from the single characters that form the basis of Chinese characters. One can understand and write combined characters well only when one has a good mastery of single characters.

　　合体字的基本结构有三种：左右结构、上下结构、包围结构。（图形中数字表示书写顺序）

There are three types of structures for combined characters：A. left and right；B. upper and lower；C. outside and inside (The number inside the boxes indicates the order of writing).

（一）左右结构

Left and Right structure

1. 左右结构 | 1 | 2 | 江、奶

Left-right characters such as 江 and 奶

2. 左中右结构 | 1 | 2 | 3 | 脚、谢

Left-middle-right characters such as 脚 and 谢

（二）上下结构

Upper and Lower structure

1. 上下结构 | 1 / 2 | 思、笔

Upper-lower characters such as 思 and 笔

2. 上中下结构 | 1 / 2 / 3 | 章、鼻

Upper-middle-lower characters such as 章 and 鼻

（三）包围结构

Outside and Inside structure

1. 全包围结构 | 1 / 2 / 3 | 回、国

Full outside-inside characters such as 回 and 国

2. 两包围结构

Two-sided outside-inside characters

(1)左上包围 床、有

The top left closing type such as 床 and 有

(2)右上包围 句、司

The top right closing type such as 句 and 司

(3)左下包围 爬、起 边、建

The lower left closing type such as 边 and 建

3. 三包围结构

Three-sided outside-inside characters

(1)上方三包围 同、问

The top three-sided characters such as 同 and 问

(2)下方三包围 凶、击

The lower three-sided characters such as 凶 and 击

(3)左方三包围 医、区

The left three-sided characters such as 医 and 区

包围结构的汉字一般先写外边,再写里边。但也有例外,如:这、凶。

Generally speaking, in writing the outside-inside type of Chinese characters, the outside part should be given before the inside part. But there are exceptions such as 这 and 凶.

合体字还有一些复杂的结构,大部分是以上基本结构的组合或变形,主要的书写也多遵循先左后右,先上后下,先外后内的规律。如:

Some combined characters are struturally complicated, but the majority of them are the combination or alteration of the above-mentioned patterns. They are written in the order of left-right, upper-lower or outside-inside formation. For example:

1	2			1	2				1					1	2			1	3	
	3	语		2	3	部		2	3	宿				3		想		2	4	能

根据《汉字信息字典》统计,左右结构的字占总字数的 64.9%,其次是上下结构的字占 21.1%,由此可见,左右结构和上下结构是汉字的两种最基本的结构形式。

The statistics of *An Informative Dictionary of Chinese Characters* show that the left-right type of characters account for 64.9% of the total; the upper-lower type of characters accounts for 21.1%. Obviously those two types of structures are the basic formation of Chinese characters.

生字词表
List of New Characters and Words

1.休	xiū	to rest, to stop
休息	xiūxi	to have a rest
2.体	tǐ	body
体重	tǐzhòng	body weight
3.什	shén	
什么	shénme	what
4.候	hòu	to wait
时候	shíhou	time
有时候	yǒu shíhou	sometimes
气候	qìhòu	climate

5.	件	jiàn	piece
	条件	tiáojiàn	condition
	文件	wénjiàn	document
6.	住	zhù	to live in/at⋯⋯
	住院	zhù yuàn	to hospitalize
7.	借	jiè	to borrow
8.	俩	liǎ	two
9.	化	huà	to change, to transform
	文化	wénhuà	culture
10.	做	zuò	to do, to make
11.	健	jiàn	healthy, strong
	健康	jiànkāng	health
12.	但	dàn	but
	但是	dànshì	but
13.	假	①jià	leave, holiday, vacation
	请假	qǐngjià	to ask for leave
		②jiǎ	false
	说假话	shuō jiǎhuà	to tell a lie
14.	会	huì	can, to meet, meeting
	一会儿	yíhuìr	a short while
	晚会	wǎnhuì	evening party
	机会	jīhuì	opportunity
15.	全	quán	whole, complete
	全校	quán xiào	whole school
	全体	quántǐ	all, entire
16.	舍	shè	dormitory
	宿舍	sùshè	dormitory
17.	每	měi	every
	每天	měi tiān	every day
	每年	měi nián	every year
18.	复	fù	compound
	复习	fùxí	to review
	复印	fùyìn	to photocopy
	复杂	fùzá	complex

19. 言	yán	language
方言	fāngyán	dialect
20. 说	shuō	to say
听说	tīngshuō	to be told
小说	xiǎoshuō	novel
21. 话	huà	speech
打电话	dǎ diànhuà	to make a phone call
会话	huìhuà	dialogue
22. 请	qǐng	to invite, request, please
请进	qǐng jìn	Come in, please!
23. 该	gāi	should
应该	yīnggāi	should
24. 谁	shuí	who
25. 谢	xiè	to thank
谢谢	xièxie	thanks
26. 词	cí	word
生词	shēngcí	new word
27. 课	kè	lesson
课文	kèwén	text
28. 认	rèn	to recognize
认真	rènzhēn	carefully
认为	rènwéi	to think, to consider
29. 识	shí	to know
认识	rènshi	to know, knowledge
30. 试	shì	to try, examination
试一试	shì yi shì	to have a try
考试	kǎoshì	examination
31. 读	dú	to read
读书	dú shū	to read (a book)
32. 记	jì	to remember, to write down
笔记	bǐjì	notes
日记	rìjì	diary
记住	jìzhù	to remember firmly

33. 谈	tán	to talk, to chat
谈话	tánhuà	to discuss, talks
34. 诉	sù	to tell, to accuse
告诉	gàosu	to tell, to warn
35. 译	yì	to translate
翻译	fānyì	to translate, to interpret translator, interpreter
36. 让	ràng	to let, to allow, to give away

生字的结构和书写

The Structures and Writing of the New Characters

亻   单立人旁   dān lì rén páng   The Radical of 亻

亻	亻												

　　"亻"是由"人"演变而来的。象形字"人"见上册第52页。"人"在左边写做"亻"，称为"单立人旁"，在上边写做"入"，称为"人字头"，有时也写做"ク"，称为"卧人头"。包含"亻"的偏旁往往与人和人的行为、动作、感情有关。

The characters with the pictophonetic radical 亻 derived from 人 are generally related to people, human activities and feelings. When standing on the left of a character it is written as 亻, known as "literally means sign of a single standing man". When used on the top of a character it is written as 人, known as "a man top-sign", or as ク known as "a lying man sign".

休   xiū   to rest, to stop

休息   xiūxi   to have a rest

①亻   ②木

2 体　　tǐ　body

体重　tǐzhòng　body weight
①亻　②本

3 什　　shén

什么　shénme　what
①亻　②十

4 候　　hòu　to wait

时候　shíhou　time
有时候　yǒu shíhou　sometimes
气候　qìhòu　climate
①亻　②丨　③⊐ 「 ⊐　④矢

5 件　　jiàn　piece

条件　tiáojiàn　condition
文件　wénjiàn　document
①亻　②牛

6 住　　zhù　to live in/at……

住院　zhù yuàn　to hospitalize
①亻　②主(zhǔ) 丶 主

7 借　　jiè　to borrow

①亻　②+③昔

8 俩　　liǎ　two

①亻　②两

⑨ 化

huà　to change, to transform

文化　wénhuà　culture

1	2

①亻　②匕

⑩ 做

zuò　to do, to make

1	2	3

①亻　②古 十 古　③攵 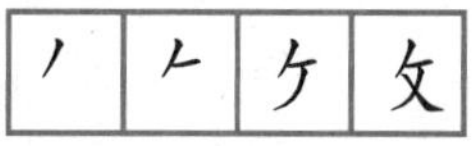

⑪ 健

jiàn　healthy, strong

健康　jiànkāng　health

1	2 (above), 3 (below)

①亻　②+③建(jiàn) 

⑫ 但

dàn　but

但是　dànshì　but

1	2

①亻　②旦(dàn) 日 旦

⑬ 假

①jià　leave, holiday, vacation

请假　qǐngjià　to ask for leave

②jiǎ　false

说假话　shuō jiǎhuà　to tell a lie

1	2	3 (above), 4 (below)

①亻　② 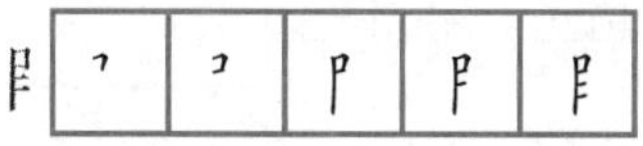　③ 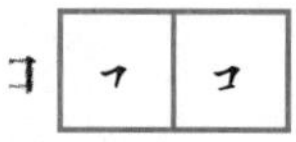　④又

人

人字头　rén zì tóu　The Radical of 人

人	人										

⑭ 会

huì　can, to meet, meeting

一会儿　yíhuìr　a short while

晚会　wǎnhuì　evening party

机会　jīhuì　opportunity

1
2

①人　②云

⑮ 全　quán　whole, complete

1
2

全校　quán xiào　whole school
全体　quántǐ　all, entire
①人　②王

⑯ 舍　shè　dormitory

1
2
3

宿舍　sùshè　dormitory
①人　②干　③口

⺊　卧人头　wò rén tóu　The Radical of ⺊

⺊	⺊										

⑰ 每　měi　every

1
2

每天　měi tiān　every day
每年　měi nián　every year
①⺊　②母

⑱ 复　fù　compound

1
2
3

复习　fùxí　to review
复印　fùyìn　to photocopy
复杂　fùzá　complex

①⺊　②日　③夂

ノ	ク	夂

讠　言字旁　yán zì páng　The Radical of 讠

讠	讠										

"讠"是"言"演化而来的。"言"字做形旁的字多与说话有关,言字旁在字的左侧,简化成"讠"。

The characters with the pictophonetic radical 讠 derived from the self-explanatory character 言 are often related to speech. When standing on the left of a character, it is simplified as 讠.

⑲ 言 yán language

方言 fāngyán dialect

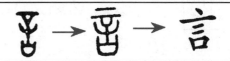

在古字"舌"上加一横，表示声音是从这儿发出的。

> The ancient written form of 言 is in the shape of a human tongue with a horizontal, indicating the position where a sound is uttered.

言 言 言 言 言 言 言

上横长，下面两横短。

> Of the three horizontals, the top one is the longest, the rest two underneath are shorter.

⑳ 说 shuō to say

听说 tīngshuō to be told

小说 xiǎoshuō novel

$\begin{array}{c}1\begin{array}{|c|}2\\\hline3\end{array}\end{array}$

①讠 ②+③兑(duì) 丶 丷 台 兑 兑

㉑ 话 huà speech

打电话 dǎ diànhuà to make a phone call

会话 huìhuà dialogue

1 2

①讠 ②舌

㉒ 请 qǐng to invite, request, please

请进 qǐng jìn Come in, please!

1 2

①讠 ②青

23 该 gāi should

应该 yīnggāi should

1	2

①讠 ②亥

24 谁 shuí who

①讠 ②隹(zhuī)

1	2

25 谢 xiè to thank

谢谢 xièxie thanks

1	2	3

①讠 ②身 | ′ | ′ | 亻 | 亻 | 自 | 身 | 身 | ③寸

26 词 cí word

生词 shēngcí new word

1	2

①讠 ②司(sī) | ㄱ | ㄱ | 司 |

27 课 kè lesson

课文 kèwén text

1	2

①讠 ②果

28 认 rèn to recognize

认真 rènzhēn carefully

认为 rènwéi to think, to consider

1	2

①讠 ②人

29 识 shí to know

认识 rènshi to know, knowledge

1	2

①讠 ②只(zhī) | 口 | 只 |

30 试   shì   to try, examination

试一试   shì yi shì   to have a try

考试   kǎoshì   examination

①讠   ②式(shì) | 一 | 弍 | 式 | 式 |

31 读   dú   to read

读书   dú shū   to read (a book)

①讠   ②卖

32 记   jì   to remember, to write down

笔记   bǐjì   notes

日记   rìjì   diary

记住   jìzhù   to remember firmly

①讠   ②己

33 谈   tán   to talk, to chat

谈话   tánhuà   to discuss, talks

①讠   ②炎(yán) | 火 | 炎 |

34 诉   sù   to tell, to accuse

告诉   gàosu   to tell, to warn

①讠   ②斥 | 斤 | 斥 |

35 译   yì   to translate

翻译   fānyì   to translate, to interpret, translator, interpreter

①讠   ②𢆉 | ㇇ | 又 | 圣 | 圣 | 𢆉 |

36 让   ràng   to let, to allow, to give away

①讠   ②上

认读词、词组和句子

Read the Following Words，Phrases and Sentences

一、认读词、词组
Read the Following Words and Phrases.

休：休息　午休　休假

体：身体　体重　人体　体力　物体　集体　气体

件：一件衣服　一件毛衣　一件礼物

住：住校　住宿　住址　站住

借：借书　借钱　借自行车

假：(jià)请假　假期　假日　(jiǎ)假山　假话　假人
　　假牙　假手

俩：父子俩　父女俩　母子俩　母女俩　他们俩
　　你们俩

会：一会儿　会见　晚会　开会　会场　会话

全：全球　全国　全市　全校　全班　全体　全面
　　全力　全场　全年　全天　全民　全身

每：每天　每年　每个月　每小时　每分钟　每星期
　　每人

复：复习　复印　复印机

说：说话　听说　小说　说明

话：电话　谈话　说话　听话　说大话

请：请坐　请进　请喝咖啡　请问　请假

词：生词　词典　动词　名词

课：课文　课本　上课　下课　课上　课下　第一课

认：认真　认识

试：考试　口试　笔试　面试　试一下

记:记住　笔记　日记　笔记本　记生词　记下来
　　记不住
读:读物　读者　读音　读大学
让:让步　让路　让开　请让一下

二、认读下列句子

Read the Following Sentences.

1. 你每天什么时候做作业？晚上几点睡觉？

2. 昨天的口语考试难不难？

3. 我听说你翻译了一本中文小说,能不能让我看一下？

4. 上课的时候,我每天记笔记,下课以后认真复习,做作
　　业,读课文,这样,我觉得汉语越学越容易了。

5. 老师昨天告诉我们,明天不考试了。

6. 我不认识王明,但是听说过这个人。

7. 这些笔记你能不能帮我复印一下？

8. 金成汉回国了,他请了一个星期的假。

9. 你住几楼？你们的宿舍条件怎么样？

10. A:昨天的晚会谁没来？
　　　B:山本没来,他前天住院了。

11. 他身高一米七五,体重七十五公斤,身体非常健康。

12. 中国有很多方言,有时候你跟说方言的中国人谈话,
　　　没有人翻译,你不知道他们在说什么。

13. A:请进！小王刚才打电话来,让你在宿舍等他一会
　　　　儿。你先请坐吧。
　　　B:谢谢！我是来向他借书的。

14. 孩子说了假话,父母应该不应该打孩子？

15. 考试前全校放假休息一天。

第十五课

 基本知识
Rudiments of Chinese Characters

汉字的偏旁(四)
The Radicals of Chinese Characters (D)

汉字的一些偏旁位置比较灵活,同一个偏旁在不同的字里,偏旁位置可以不同。如:

The positions of some radicals in Chinese characters are flexible. One radical can be put in different positions in different characters, for example:

又:支	土:堂	工:贡	口:喝
圣	在	红	号
难	地	功	名
发	去	空	知

但在一个汉字中,偏旁的位置是固定的,如果偏旁的位置调换一下,可能就变成了另一个字,也可能就变成了错字。如:

However the position of a radical is fixed in a Chinese character. It will be a different or even wrong character if its position is shifted, for example:

另(lìng)——加(jiā) 部(bù)——陪(péi)
古(gǔ)——叶(yè) 旧(jiù)——旦(dàn)

所以学习汉字时,不仅要记住它们的偏旁,还要记住这些偏旁的位置。

Therefore, learners should memorize not only the radical but also its position when they learn a Chinese character.

另外，还有一些偏旁，为了适应合体结构的要求，不同的位置，有不同的变体，但这些不同变体的偏旁所包含的意思差不多。如：

What's more, some radicals may be subject to modifications to meet the needs of different combined characters, known as "variations". The radicals of the various variations at different positions imply similar meanings, for example：

炼：火（火字旁）　　感：心（心字底）　　拿：手（手字底）
照：灬（四点底）　　慢：忄（竖心旁）　　报：扌（提手旁）
　　　　　　　　　　慕：小（竖心底）　　看：龵（手字头）

生字词表
List of New Characters and Words

1. 意	yì	meaning
意见	yìjiàn	opinion
同意	tóngyì	to agree
2. 思	sī	to think
意思	yìsi	meaning
不好意思	bù hǎoyìsi	to be shy
没意思	méi yìsi	boring, uninteresting
有意思	yǒu yìsi	interesting
3. 想	xiǎng	to think
想念	xiǎngniàn	to miss
4. 感	gǎn	to feel, to move
感冒	gǎnmào	to have a cold
感谢	gǎnxiè	to thank
5. 念	niàn	to read
念课文	niàn kèwén	to read a text
6. 忘	wàng	to forget
忘记	wàngjì	to forget

7. 怎	zěn	how
怎么	zěnme	how
8. 息	xī	breath
休息	xiūxi	to take a rest
9. 急	jí	in a hurry, anxious
着急	zháojí	to worry about, to be worried about
10. 忽	hū	sudden, to ignore
忽然	hūrán	suddenly
11. 愿	yuàn	to want, to hope, to be willing
愿意	yuànyì	to be willing to
12. 快	kuài	quick, happy, sharp
快乐	kuàilè	happy
13. 慢	màn	slow
14. 惯	guàn	to get used to
习惯	xíguàn	habit
15. 怪	guài	strange
奇怪	qíguài	strange
16. 忙	máng	busy
大忙人	dàmángrén	busy person
17. 懂	dǒng	to understand
18. 情	qíng	feeling, love, circumstance
情况	qíngkuàng	situation
19. 拿	ná	to take
20. 拳	quán	fist
太极拳	tàijíquán	shadow boxing
21. 打	dǎ	to beat, to play, to make
打听	dǎting	to inquire
打电话	dǎ diànhuà	to make a phone call
打工	dǎgōng	to do manual work
打的	dǎ dí	to take a taxi
22. 找	zhǎo	to look for

23. 把	bǎ	[preposition transposing the object before the verb], (of an instrument with a handle)
24. 搬	bān	to move
搬家	bān jiā	to move (house)
25. 报	bào	to report
报纸	bàozhǐ	newspaper
报名	bào míng	to enroll, to sign up
26. 换	huàn	to change
交换	jiāohuàn	to exchange
27. 挤	jǐ	crowded
28. 操	cāo	exercise
操场	cāochǎng	sports ground
29. 接	jiē	to receive, to meet
接电话	jiē diànhuà	to answer the phone
接人	jiē rén	to meet somebody
30. 切	qiē	to cut
切菜	qiē cài	to cut vegetables
31. 刻	kè	to cut, a quarter (of an hour), moment
一刻钟	yí kèzhōng	a quarter
立刻	lìkè	immediately
32. 到	dào	to arrive, until, up to
感到	gǎndào	to feel
找到	zhǎodào	to find
迟到	chídào	to be late
33. 别	bié	other, don't
别的	biéde	another
别人	biérén	others
34. 刚	gāng	just
刚才	gāngcái	just now
35. 刮	guā	to blow
刮风	guā fēng	The wind blows
36. 色	sè	colour
白色	báisè	white

生字的结构和书写

The Structures and Writing of the New Characters

心　　心字底　xīn zì dǐ　The Radical of 心

象形字"心"见上册第53页。"心"做偏旁,在字的下面时写做"心",称为"心字底";在字的左侧时写做"忄",叫"竖心旁";有时在字的下边写做"小",称为"竖心底"。"心"做偏旁的汉字多与人的思想及心理活动有关。

The pictographic script 心 (see page 53, Textbook I) as a radical is often related to thinking or state of mind. When standing on the left of a character it is written as 忄, known as "a vertical heart sign". When used at the bottom of a character it is written as 心, known as "a bottom heart sign", or written as 小, known as "a vertical heart bottom sign".

1 意　yì　meaning

1
2
3

意见　yìjiàn　opinion
同意　tóngyì　to agree
①＋②音　③心

2 思　sī　to think

1
2

意思　yìsi　meaning
不好意思　bù hǎoyìsi　to be shy
没意思　méi yìsi　boring, uninteresting
有意思　yǒu yìsi　interesting
①田　②心

3 想　xiǎng　to think

1
2

想念　xiǎngniàn　to miss
①相　②心

4 感 gǎn to feel, to move

感冒 gǎnmào to have a cold
感谢 gǎnxiè to thank
①咸(xián) 一 厂 厂 厂 咸 咸 咸 ②心

5 念 niàn to read

念课文 niàn kèwén to read a text
①今 ②心

6 忘 wàng to forget

忘记 wàngjì to forget
①亡(wáng) 丶 亠 亡 ②心

7 怎 zěn how

怎么 zěnme how
①乍 ②心

8 息 xī breath

休息 xiūxi to take a rest
①自 ②心

9 急 jí in a hurry, anxious

着急 zháojí to worry about, to be worried about
①⺈ ②彐 フ ⼹ 彐 ③心

10 忽 hū sudden, to ignore

忽然 hūrán suddenly
①勿(wù) ②心

⑪ 愿　yuàn　to want, to hope, to be willing

愿意　yuànyì　to be willing to

①＋②原(yuán) 厂 厉 原　③心

忄　竖心旁　shù xīn páng　The Radical of 忄

忄	忄	忄									

⑫ 快　kuài　quick, happy, sharp

快乐　kuàilè　happy

①忄　②夬

⑬ 慢　màn　slow

①忄　②日　③罒 丶 冖 冖 冖 罒　④又

⑭ 惯　guàn　to get used to

习惯　xíguàn　habit

①忄　②＋③贯(guàn) ﹂ 口 皿 毌 毌 毌 贯 贯

⑮ 怪　guài　strange

奇怪　qíguài　strange

①忄　②又　③土

⑯ 忙　máng　busy

大忙人　dàmángrén　busy person

①忄　②亡

17 懂　dǒng　to understand

①忄　②＋③董(dǒng)

一	忄	艹	艹	苎	芦	苜	苦	苗	莗	董	董

18 情　qíng　feeling，love，circumstance

情况　qíngkuàng　situation

①忄　②青

手　手字部　shǒu zì bù　The Radical of 手

象形字"手"见上册第63页。"手"做形旁的字多与手的动作有关，"手"在字的下边写做"手"；"手"字做字的左偏旁时写做"扌"，叫做"提手旁"；有时"手"还可在字的上边，写做"龵"，叫做"手字头"。

The pictographic script 手（see page 63，Textbook I）as a radical is often related to the movement of a hand. When standing at the bottom of a character it is written as 手. When used on the left of a character it is written as 扌，known as "a hand sign". When standing on the top of a character it is written as 龵，known as "hand top-sign".

19 拿　ná　to take

①合　②手

20 拳　quán　fist

太极拳　tàijíquán　shadow boxing

①㐵 | 丶 | 丷 | 丷 | 丷 | 半 | 㐵 | ②手

扌　提手旁　tí shǒu páng　The Radical of 扌

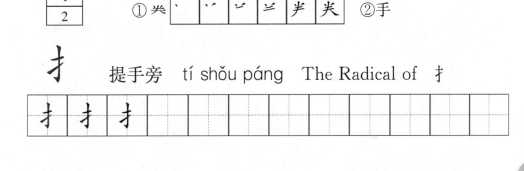

21 打

| 1 | 2 |

dǎ   to beat, to play, to make

打听   dǎting   to inquire
打电话   dǎ diànhuà   to make a phone call
打工   dǎgōng   to do manual work
打的   dǎ dí   to take a taxi

①扌   ②丁(dīng) | 一 | 丁 |

22 找

| 1 | 2 |

zhǎo   to look for

①扌   ②戈(gē) | 一 | 弋 | 戈 | 戈 |

23 把

| 1 | 2 |

bǎ   [preposition transposing the object before the verb],
(of an instrument with a handle)
①扌   ②巴

24 搬

| 1 | 2 | 3 |
| | | 4 |

bān   to move

搬家   bān jiā   to move (house)
①扌
②+③+④般(bān) | ′ | ⺁ | 刀 | 夯 | 舟 | 舟 | 舟几 | 般 |

25 报

| 1 | 2 |
| | 3 |

bào   to report

报纸   bàozhǐ   newspaper
报名   bào míng   to enroll, to sign up
①扌   ②+③⺆ | フ | ⼝ | ⻖ | 𠬝 |

26 换

| 1 | 2 |
| | 3 |

huàn   to change

交换   jiāohuàn   to exchange
①扌   ②+③奂(huàn) | ′ | ⺈ | ⺈ | 𠂊 | 𠂊 | 奂 | 奂 |

27 挤

| 1 | 2 |

jǐ   crowded

①扌   ②齐(qí) | 文 | 齐 | 齐 |

28 操　　cāo　exercise

操场　cāochǎng　sports ground

①扌　②品(pǐn) [口][品][品]　③木

29 接　　jiē　to receive, to meet

接电话　jiē diànhuà　to answer the phone

接人　jiē rén　to meet somebody

①扌　②立　③女

刀　　刀字部　dāo zì bù　The Radical of 刀

象形字"刀"见上册第106页。"刀"字做形旁的字多与刀有关。"刀"在字的右侧时常写做"刂",叫"立刀边";在字的右侧有时也写做"刀",叫"刀字边";在字的上部写做"勹",叫"刀字头"。

The pictographic script 刀 (see page 106, Textbook I) as a radical is often related to knife. When standing on the right of a character it is written as 刂, known as "a vertical knife sign"; when on the right, sometimes it is written as 刀, known as "a knife side-sign"; when used on the top it is written as 勹, known as "a knife top-sign".

30 切　　qiē　to cut

切菜　qiē cài　to cut vegetables

①七 [一][七]　②刀

刂　　立刀边　lì dāo biān　The Radical of 刂

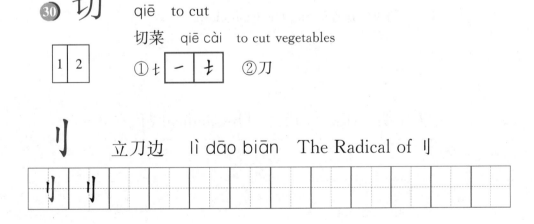

31 刻   kè   to cut , a quarter of an hour , moment

一刻钟   yí kèzhōng   a quarter
立刻   lìkè   immediately
①亥   ②刂

1	2

32 到   dào   to arrive , until , up to

感到   gǎndào   to feel
找到   zhǎodào   to find
迟到   chídào   to be late

①至 一 丆 至 至 至 至   ②刂

1	2

33 别   bié   other , don't

别的   biéde   another
别人   biérén   others

①＋②另（lìng） 口 另   ③刂

1	3
2	

34 刚   gāng   just

刚才   gāngcái   just now
①冈（gāng） 丨 冂 冈 冈   ②刂

1	2

35 刮   guā   to blow

刮风   guā fēng   The wind blows.
①舌   ②刂

1	2

ク   刀字头   dāo zì tóu   The Radical of ク

36 色   sè   colour

白色   báisè   white
①ク   ②巴

1	
2	

认读词、词组和句子
Read the Following Words，Phrases and Sentences

一、认读词、词组
Read the Following Words and Phrases.

意：意见　同意　意思　不好意思

思：思考　思念　思想

想：想念　心想　回想　料想

念：念书　纪念　念念不忘

忘：忘我　健忘　难忘　忘年交

感：感冒　感谢　感想

急：急忙　急用　心急　十万火急

愿：心愿　意愿　自愿　但愿　情愿

快：快车　快餐　快刀　飞快　快乐

慢：慢车　慢走　快慢

情：情况　感情　情人　情书　热情　心情　同情
　　爱情

打：打算　打电话　打球　打篮球　打羽毛球
　　打太极拳　打听　打开　打字

怪：怪人　怪物　怪话　怪事(shì)　难怪　见怪
　　千奇百怪

搬：搬家　搬桌子　搬东西　搬走　搬出去

报：报纸　日报　晚报　早报　球报

换：换车　换钱　换一个

到：来到　找到

找：找人　找车　找工作　找东西　找你钱
别：别的　别人　别去　别来　别走　别出去

二、认读下列句子
Read the Following Sentences.

1. 今天他感冒了，有点儿发烧，不能来上课了，请假一天。
2. 现在正在刮大风，下大雨，你别出去买报纸了。
3. 刚来的时候，我们不太习惯北京的天气，但是现在慢慢习惯了。
4. 每天早上六点，操场那儿可以学打太极拳，你去吗？
5. 你刚才说得太快了，我没有听懂，请你慢慢儿说，可以吗？
6. 先休息一刻钟，等一会儿我们再念课文。
7. 不好意思，我太忙了，忘了昨天是你的生日，今天我买了一个生日礼物，祝你生日快乐。
8. 刚才他去银行换钱，回来以后又去操场锻炼身体了。
9. 地铁太挤了，我们打的去吧。
10. 你同不同意我的意见，愿不愿意把你的意见告诉我？
11. 你是个大忙人，每天都要打工，怎么会有时间(shíjiān, time)来看我？
12. 小王刚才打电话来，他很着急，让你立刻上他那儿去。
13. 昨天切菜的时候，我把手切破(pò, broken)了。
14. 我昨天找人打听了一下，他已经搬家了，不住那儿了。
15. A：奇怪，我那件白色的上衣呢，找了半天也没找到。
    B：你别找了，我忽然想起来了，上星期你把你的衣服送(sòng, to send)到洗衣店去了，还没拿回来呢。

第十六课

基本知识
Rudiments of Chinese Characters

汉字的书写(四)
The Writing of Chinese Characters (D)

除了包含横笔和捺笔的部件在做偏旁时,笔画有变化以外,还有一些部件中的笔画也有变化。

Apart from the horizontal and right-falling strokes, other strokes are also subject to modifications when used as the components of radicals.

1. 最后一笔是竖的部件,写在字的左上方(或左边)时,竖有时写做撇。如:

If the final stroke of a component is a vertical, it is sometimes written as a left-falling stroke when used on the top left(or the left) of a character. For example:

羊 → 𦍌 : 着
辛 → 𠭇 : 辣

2. 竖钩的下面还有笔画或部件时,竖钩写做竖。如:

A vertical hook under which there is another stroke or a component should be written as a vertical. For example:

小 → 小 : 少
可 → 可 : 哥

含有竖钩的偏旁写在字的左上方(或左边)时,竖钩写做撇。如:

A vertical hook should be written as a left-falling stroke when used on the top left(or the left) of a character as a radical. For example:

手 → 手 : 看

3."月"做部件,写在字的左边或右边时,都写成"月",但当它写在字的下方时,第一笔撇写成竖。如:

月 remains unchanged when used on the left or right of a character as a radical, but its left-falling stroke should change into a vertical stroke when used at the lower part of a character. For example:

有:ナ十月　　胃:田十月
青:龶十月　　能:厶十月十匕十匕

4."雨"做部件,它下边还有别的部件时,第二笔竖写成点,第三笔横折钩写成横钩。如:

When 雨 functions as a component above another component of a character, its second stroke should be changed from a vertical to a dot, and its third stroke should be changed from a horizontal turning with a hook to a horizontal hook. For example:

雨 → 雪 : 雪

5. 有的部件在做左偏旁(或它的右边还有别的部件)时,它的末笔横的长度缩短。如:

When functioning as a left radical (or with an accompanied constituent on the right side), the length of the final stroke of a component should be shortened. For example:

女 → 女 : 奶
数(娄:米十女)
身 → 身 : 躺
舟 → 舟 : 般

生字词表
List of New Characters and Words

1.	雪	xuě	snow
	下雪	xià xuě	to snow
	滑雪	huá xuě	skiing
2.	雷	léi	thunder
	打雷	dǎléi	to thunder
3.	零	líng	zero
	零下	língxià	below zero
4.	躺	tǎng	to lie
5.	躲	duǒ	to hide
	躲开	duǒkāi	to hide from
6.	舟	zhōu	boat
7.	船	chuán	boat
	划船	huá chuán	to row a boat
8.	航	háng	to sail
	航空	hángkōng	aviation
	航班	hángbān	flight number, scheduled flight
9.	般	bān	like, kind
	一般	yìbān	usual
10.	她	tā	she
	她们	tāmen	they (famale)
11.	姐	jiě	elder sister
	姐姐	jiějie	elder sister
	小姐	xiǎojiě	miss, young lady
12.	妹	mèi	younger sister
	妹妹	mèimei	younger sister
13.	妈	mā	mother
	妈妈	māma	mother
14.	姓	xìng	surname
	姓名	xìngmíng	name

15.	妻	qī	wife
	妻子	qīzi	wife
16.	要	yào	to want
	要是	yàoshi	if
17.	着	①zhe	(an aspectual particle)
	走着去	zǒuzhe qù	to go on foot
		②zháo	
	着急	zháojí	to be worried
18.	差	chà	to fall short of
	差不多	chàbuduō	almost
19.	期	qī	term, prescribed length of time
	学期	xuéqī	semester
20.	朋	péng	friend
	朋友	péngyou	friend
21.	肥	féi	fat, loose, wide
	减肥	jiǎnféi	lose weight
22.	胖	pàng	fat
	胖子	pàngzi	plump person
23.	胃	wèi	stomach
24.	青	qīng	green
	青年	qīngnián	youth
25.	服	fú	clothes, to take (medicine)
	衣服	yīfu	clothes
26.	脏	①zāng	dirty
	脏衣服	zāng yīfu	dirty clothes
		②zàng	internal organ
	心脏	xīnzàng	heart
27.	脱	tuō	to take off
28.	脚	jiǎo	foot
29.	脸	liǎn	face
	脸色	liǎnsè	look, complexion

30.	脑	nǎo	brain
	电脑	diànnǎo	computer
	笔记本电脑	bǐjìběn diànnǎo	laptop
31.	爸	bà	dad, father
	爸爸	bàba	dad, father
32.	爷	yé	grandpa
	爷爷	yéye	grandpa
33.	夕	xī	evening
	夕阳	xīyáng	setting sun
34.	岁	suì	age, year
	岁数	suìshu	age
35.	梦	mèng	dream
	做梦	zuòmèng	to dream
	梦见	mèngjiàn	to see in a dream
36.	外	wài	outside
	外国	wàiguó	foreign country
	外语	wàiyǔ	foreign language
	老外	lǎowài	foreigner
37.	名	míng	name, famous
	名字	míngzi	name
	名片	míngpiàn	calling card
	有名	yǒumíng	famous, well-known
38.	封	fēng	to seal
	一封信	yì fēng xìn	a letter
39.	时	shí	time, hour
	小时	xiǎoshí	hour
	时间	shíjiān	(the concept of) time, (the duration of) time

生字的结构和书写

The Structures and Writing of the New Characters

雨 　雨字头　yǔ zì tóu　The Radical of 雨

雨	雨	雨	雨	雨	雨	雨	雨				

象形字"雨"见上册第 75 页。"雨"做形旁的字一般与下雨或气象情况有关,雨字头在字的上部,写做"雨",第二笔竖改为点,第三笔横折钩改为横钩。

The pictographic script 雨 (see page 75, Textbook I) as a radical is generally related to rainfall or rainy weather. When standing on the top of a character, it is written as 雨 with the second stroke of the left vertical replaced by a dot, and the third stroke of the horizontal turning with a hook replaced by a horizontal hook.

1 雪　xuě　snow

下雪　xià xuě　to snow

滑雪　huá xuě　skiing

①雨　②ヨ | ㄱ | ㄱ | ヨ |

2 雷　léi　thunder

打雷　dǎléi　to thunder

①雨　②田

3 零　líng　zero

零下　língxià　below zero

①雨　②令(lìng) | ノ | 八 | 八 | 今 | 令 |

身　身字旁　shēn zì páng　The Radical of 身

身	身	身	身	身	身	身					

象形字"身"见上册第116页。"身"做形旁的汉字多与身体有关,身字旁在字的左侧,写做"身",末笔撇不出头。

The pictographic script 身 (see page 116, Texbook Ⅰ) as a radical is often related to human body. When standing on the left of a character it is written as 身. Its final left-falling stroke does not go across the vertical part of the horizontal turning with a hook.

4 躺　tǎng　to lie

①身　②+③尚(shàng)

丨	丬	业	业	严	兴	尚	尚

1	2
	3

5 躲　duǒ　to hide

躲开　duǒkāi　to hide from

①身　②朵(duǒ)

几	朵

1	2

舟　舟字旁　zhōu zì páng　The Radical of 舟

6 舟　zhōu　boat

古字像一只弯弯的小船。

The ancient written form of 舟 is in the shape of a little boat.

舟 | 舟 | 舟 | 舟 | 舟 | 舟 | | | | |

第一笔是"短撇",第二笔是"竖撇",中间的"横"在田字格中间的横线上,上下两点同一方向。

The first stroke of 舟 is a left short falling, and its second stroke is a left-vertical falling. The horizontal stroke should be placed on the central line of a square printed on the writing paper. The two dots are arranged up and down in the same direction.

"舟"做形旁的字多与船有关。舟字旁在字的左侧,写做"舟",第五笔"横"右边不出头。

The pictographic script 舟 as a radical is often associated with boat. When standing on the left of a character it is written as 舟. Its fifth stroke of the horizontal stroke does not go across the vertical part of the horizontal turning with a hook.

7 船 chuán boat

划船 huá chuán to row a boat

① 舟 ② 㕣

8 航 háng to sail

航班 hángbān flight number, scheduled flight
航空 hángkōng aviation

① 舟 ②+③亢(kàng) ` | 亠 | 广 | 亢

9 般 bān like, kind

一般 yìbān usual

① 舟 ② 殳

女

女字旁　nǚ zì páng　The Radical of 女

象形字"女"见上册第 52 页。"女"做形旁的字多与女性有关。女字旁一般在字的左侧,写做"女",末笔"横"跟第二笔"撇"相接。有时也可在字的下边,写做"女"。

The pictographic script 女 (see page 52, Textbook I) as a radical is often related to woman. When standing on the left of a character, it is written as 女 with its final horizontal stroke connecting with the second left-falling stroke. Sometimes it is also used at the lower part of a character without changing its writing.

10 她　tā　she

她们　tāmen　they (famale)
①女　②也

| 1 | 2 |

11 姐　jiě　elder sister

姐姐　jiějie　elder sister
小姐　xiǎojiě　miss, young lady
①女　②且(qiě)　| 丨 | 冂 | 冃 | 日 | 且 |

| 1 | 2 |

12 妹　mèi　younger sister

妹妹　mèimei　younger sister
①女　②未(wèi)　| 一 | 二 | 丰 | 牛 | 未 |

| 1 | 2 |

13 妈　mā　mother

妈妈　māmā　mother
①女　②马

| 1 | 2 |

14 姓　xìng　surname

姓名　xìngmíng　name
①女　②生

| 1 | 2 |

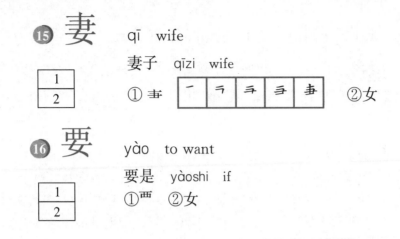

15 妻　qī　wife

妻子　qīzi　wife

1
2

①妻　一　㇕　㇌　㇍　妻　②女

16 要　yào　to want

要是　yàoshi　if

1
2

①覀　②女

羊　羊字旁　yáng zì páng　The Radical of 羊

象形字"羊"见上册第 89 页。"羊"做形旁的字多与羊有关。羊字旁位置较灵活。在字的左侧或左上侧写做"⺶"，末笔"竖"改为"撇"。在字的上部有时写做"⺷"。有时也可在字的右侧。

> The pictographic script 羊（see page 89, Textbook I）as a radical is often related to sheep or goat. The positions of 羊 as a radical are flexible. When used on the leftor top left of a character, it is written as ⺶ with its final vertical stroke replaced by a left-falling stroke. As a top radical it is sometimes written as ⺷. It can also be used on the right of a character.

17 着

①zhe　（an aspectual particle）

走着去　zǒuzhe qù　to go on foot

②zháo

着急　zháojí　to be worried

1	
	2

①⺶　丶　丷　⺌　兰　羊　②目

18 差　chà　to fall short of

差不多　chàbuduō　almost
①羊　②工

月　月字旁　yuè zì páng　The Radical of　月

象形字"月"见上册第72页。"月"做形旁的字多与时间、光亮有关,一般在字的右侧,也叫"右月旁"。月字旁在字的左侧,是"肉"做偏旁的简化,一般与肉体有关,也叫"左月旁"或"肉月旁"。有时也可在字的下边,这时"月"的第一笔撇变竖。

> The pictographic script 月 (see page 72, Textbook I) as a radical is often connected with time or light. Generally speaking, it is used at the right side of a character, known as "a right moon sign" When used on the left of a character, it is associated with human muscle or animals' meat, therefore its modified form as a radical is considered the simplification of 肉, known as "a left moon sign" or "a muscle moon sign". Sometimes it may also be used at the lower part of a character with its first stroke of the left-falling stroke replaced by a vertical.

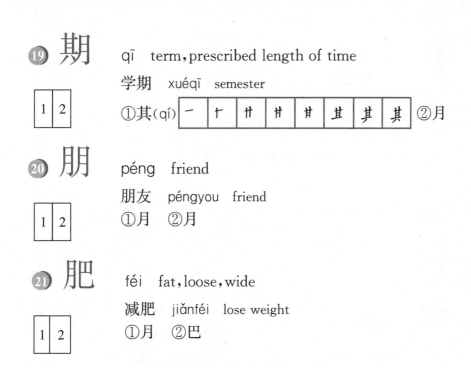

19 期　qī　term, prescribed length of time

学期　xuéqī　semester
①其(qí) 一 十 艹 艹 甘 其 其 其 ②月

20 朋　péng　friend

朋友　péngyou　friend
①月　②月

21 肥　féi　fat, loose, wide

减肥　jiǎnféi　lose weight
①月　②巴

22 胖　pàng　fat

胖子　pàngzi　plump person

①月　②半(bàn)　| 丶 | 丷 | ㅛ | 半 | 半 |

| 1 | 2 |

23 胃　wèi　stomach

①田　②月

| 1 |
| 2 |

24 青　qīng　green

青年　qīngnián　youth

①龶　②月

| 1 |
| 2 |

25 服　fú　clothes, to take (medicire)

衣服　yīfu　clothes

①月　②⻆

| 1 | 2 |

26 脏　①zāng　dirty

脏衣服　zāng yīfu　dirty clothes

②zàng　internal organ

心脏　xīnzàng　heart

①月　②庄(zhuāng)　| 广 | 庄 |

| 1 | 2 |

27 脱　tuō　to take off

①月　②兑

| 1 | 2 |

28 脚　jiǎo　foot

①月　②去　③卩 | 乛 | 卩 |

| 1 | 2 | 3 |

54

29 脸　liǎn　face

脸色　liǎnsè　look, complexion

| 1 | 2 |

①月　②金　| ノ | 人 | 人 | 仝 | 全 | 亼 | 金 |

30 脑　nǎo　brain

电脑　diànnǎo　computer

笔记本电脑　bǐjìběn diànnǎo　laptop

| 1 | 2 |

①月　②囟　| 、 | 亠 | 宀 | 文 | 区 | 囟 |

父　父字头　fù zì tóu　The Radical of 父

象形字"父"见上册第59页。"父"做形旁的字很少,一般是对男性长辈的称呼,常在字的上部,写得扁一些。

> The pictographic script 父 (see page 59, Textbook I) as a rarely used radical is generally applied as a form of address for a male senior member. It is often written flatly on the top of a character.

31 爸　bà　dad, father

爸爸　bàba　dad, father

| 1 |
| 2 |

①父　②巴

32 爷　yé　grandpa

爷爷　yéye　grandpa

| 1 |
| 2 |

①父　②卩

夕　夕字旁　xī zì páng　The Radical of 夕

33 夕　xī　evening

夕阳　xīyáng　setting sun

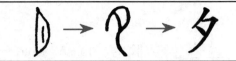

古代"夕"字中间比"月"少了一画,表示月亮露出了一半,是傍晚时分。

The ancient written form of 夕 is in the shape of 月 with one stroke missing. It indicates "dusk" at the time when the moon reveals itself partially.

第二笔"横撇"与第一笔"撇"相接。"横撇"中的撇笔较长。

The second of 夕 is a left horizontal long falling that is connected with the first left falling.

"夕"做形旁的字常与夜晚有关,"夕"做偏旁位置较灵活。

The characters with the self-explanatory character 夕 as a radical are often related to evening. It may be placed at the different positions of a character.

34 岁 suì age, year

岁数 suìshu age
①山 ②夕

35 梦 mèng dream

做梦 zuòmèng to dream
梦见 mèngjiàn to see in a dream
①+②林(lín) 木 林 ③夕

36 外 wài outside

外国 wàiguó foreign country
外语 wàiyǔ foreign language
老外 lǎowài foreigner

①夕　②卜(bǔ)　| 丨 | 卜 |

37 名　　míng　name, famous

1
2

名字　míngzi　name

名片　míngpiàn　calling card

有名　yǒumíng　famous, well-known

①夕　②口

寸　　寸字旁　cùn zì páng　The Radical of 寸

"寸"做形旁的字常跟"手"有关。"寸"做偏旁时常在字的右边或下边。

寸	寸	寸												

When functioning as a radical 寸 is often related to human hands. It can be used on the right or at the lower part of a character.

38 封　　fēng　to seal

1	2

一封信　yì fēng xìn　a letter

①圭　| 一 | 十 | 土 | 圭 | 丰 | 圭 |　②寸

39 时　　shí　time, hour

1	2

小时　xiǎoshí　hour

时间　shíjiān　(the concept of) time，(the duration of) time

①日　②寸

认读词、词组和句子

Read the Following Words，Phrases and Sentences

一、认读词、词组

Read the Following Words and Phrases.

雪：下雪　大雪　雪水　雪人　雪山　雪白　雪片

零：零上　零下　零食　零钱

船：船票　船厂　船长　木船　铁船　龙船　船上

航：航空　航天　民航　航向　起航　航行　航班

姐：姐姐　小姐　姐妹俩　空姐

期：星期　学期　短期　长期　日期　假期　时期
　　早期　中期　晚期

朋友：男朋友　女朋友　小朋友　好朋友

胖：肥胖　发胖　胖人　大胖子

服：衣服　西服　礼服　校服

脱：脱衣服　脱鞋　脱下来

脑：大脑　脑子　电脑

岁：几岁　岁数

梦：做梦　梦见　梦想　梦话

外：外国　外语　外面　外边　外衣　外文　外地
　　外交　外祖父　外祖母　国外　课外　郊外　中外
　　老外

名：名字　姓名　名片　名人　名城　名词　名酒
　　名山　名言

封：一封信　封口　封面　信封

时：时间　小时　时候　时刻　时期　时差　同时　有时

二、认读下列句子

Read the Following Sentences.

1. 下学期我想去国外的大学学习。

2. 前天下了一场大雪,昨天的天气预(yù)报说,今天零下十度(dù)。

3. 阿里的女朋友跟他生气了,这几天,她躲着不想见他。

4. 我一般下午五点以后去操场锻炼,每天差不多锻炼两个小时。

5. 别躺着看书,对眼睛不好。

6. 他妻子比较胖,衣服很难买。

7. 你的衣服太脏了,快脱下来吧。

8. 这是我的名片,电话号码和 e-mail 地址上面都有。

9. 下学期他妹妹要去外国语大学学习。

10. 东方航空公司的 CA521 航班下午四点二十分到达北京。

11. 你爷爷、奶奶今年多大岁数了?

12. 我昨天晚上做了一个梦,梦见我女朋友也来中国了。

13. A:你怎么了? 脸色很差。
    B:最近因为减肥,胃不好,心脏也不好。

14. A:昨天我给你发(fā,to send)了一封信,你看到了吗?
    B:没有,这几天我的电脑坏了。

15. A:昨天晚上下雪了,路上很滑,今天没骑车。
    B:要是走着来学校,多长时间才能到?
    A:大概半个小时吧。

第十七课

基本知识
Rudiments of Chinese Characters

查字典(一)
The Consultation of a Dictionary (A)

音序查字法
Finding Characters by Using the Phonetic Index

在学习汉语的过程中,常会用到字典、词典等工具书。怎样在这些工具书中查找汉字呢? 目前字典或词典最常用的检字法主要有三种,即音序查字法、笔画查字法、部首查字法。

> Dictionaries of Chinese characters and words are frequently used when learning Chinese. How do we look up a Chinese character in such a dictionary? There are three ways: By using the phonetic index; the index of strokes; and the index of radicals of characters.

音序查字法是按照汉字的读音来查字的方法。字典或词典中所收的字一般是按拼音的顺序来排列的,这与其他拼音文字的词典一样,使用拼音文字的外国人使用起来比较方便。

> The phonetic index is an arrangement by which characters are grouped according to their pronunciations. In a Chinese dictionary, entries are made phonetically. Those whose native language has an alphabetic system will find it convenient to use such a dictionary.

比如你知道"藏"字的发音是"cáng",如果要在《新华字典》中查"藏"字,首先你可以通过《汉语拼音音节索引》找到C,在C栏中再找"cang 仓 39","39"是"cang"这个音节在字典中的页码,翻到39页就可以看到"cang"这个音节,然后根据阴平(‒)、阳平(ˊ)、上声(ˇ)、去声(ˋ)、轻声的顺序找到"cáng",这样就很容易找到"藏"这个字了。

Suppose you know the pronunciation of 藏 is "cáng", you can find the character in the *Xinhua Dictionary of Chinese Characters* by locating "cang 仓 39"from the "C" entry of the phonetic index, then opening it to page 39, and looking up the character according to the four-tone order.

生字词表

List of New Characters and Words

1.	破	pò	broken
	书破了	shū pò le	The book was torn.
2.	矿	kuàng	mine
	矿泉水	kuàngquánshuǐ	mineral water
3.	碗	wǎn	bowl
4.	磁	cí	magnetism
	磁带	cídài	tape
5.	码	mǎ	to pile
	号码	hàomǎ	number
6.	皂	zào	soap
	香皂	xiāngzào	toilet soap
7.	泉	quán	spring
	泉水	quánshuǐ	spring water
8.	观	guān	to see, view
	参观	cānguān	to visit
9.	视	shì	to watch
	电视机	diànshìjī	TV set

10.	览	lǎn	to read, to see
	阅览室	yuèlǎnshì	reading room
11.	觉	①jiào	sleep
	睡觉	shuìjiào	to sleep
		②jué	to feel, sense
	觉得	juéde	to feel
12.	贝	bèi	shellfish
13.	贵	guì	noble, expensive
	贵姓	guìxìng	What's your name, please?
14.	货	huò	goods
	售货员	shòuhuòyuán	salesman, saleswoman
15.	费	fèi	fee, to cost
	学费	xuéfèi	tuition fee
	生活费	shēnghuófèi	living expense
16.	贸	mào	trade
	贸易	màoyì	trade
	外贸	wàimào	foreign trade
17.	贺	hè	to congratulate
	祝贺	zhùhè	to congratulate
18.	员	yuán	member
	运动员	yùndòngyuán	sportsman, sportswoman
19.	页	yè	page
	网页	wǎngyè	web page
	主页	zhǔyè	main page
20.	预	yù	in advance
	预习	yùxí	to preview
	预报	yùbào	forecast
21.	颜	yán	colour
	颜色	yánsè	colour

22. 题	tí	to inscribe
问题	wèntí	question
23. 顾	gù	to care about
照顾	zhàogù	to take care of
24. 新	xīn	new
新年	xīnnián	new year
25. 所	suǒ	therefore
所以	suǒyǐ	place
所有	suǒyǒu	all
26. 近	jìn	near
最近	zuìjìn	recent
27. 布	bù	cloth
布鞋	bù xié	cloth shoes
28. 币	bì	currency
人民币	rénmínbì	renminbi
外币	wàibì	foreign currencies
29. 市	shì	city, market
市长	shìzhǎng	mayor
超市	chāoshì	supermarket
30. 师	shī	teacher, master
老师	lǎoshī	teacher
律师	lùshī	lawyer
31. 带	dài	to bring
带来	dàilái	to bring
32. 常	cháng	often, normal
常常	chángcháng	often
33. 帮	bāng	to help
帮助	bāngzhù	to help
34. 帽	mào	hat
帽子	màozi	hat

生字的结构和书写

The Structures and Writing of the New Characters

石　　石字旁　shí zì páng　The Radical of 石

象形字"石"见上册第77页。"石"做偏旁的字多和石头及其坚硬的属性有关。石字旁一般在字的左侧。

The pictographic script 石（see page 77, Textbook I）as a radical is related to stone or solidness of something. It is generally used as a left radical.

1 破　pò　broken

书破了　shū pò le　The book was torn.

①石　②皮

1	2

2 矿　kuàng　mine

矿泉水　kuàngquánshuǐ　mineral water

①石　②广

1	2

3 碗　wǎn　bowl

①石　②宛(wǎn)

1	2

丶 丷 宀 宀 匆 夗 夗 宛

4 磁　cí　magnetism

磁带　cídài　tape

①石　②兹(zī)

1	2

丶 丷 丷 并 兹 兹 兹 兹 兹

5 码　mǎ　to pile

号码　hàomǎ　number

①石　②马

白　白字旁　bái zì páng　The Radical of 白

象形字"白"见上册第73页。"白"做形旁一般在字的左侧,有时也可以在上边。

The pictographic script 白 (see page 73, Textbook I) as a radical is often used on the left of a character, but sometimes it also appears on the top of a character.

6 皂　zào　soap

香皂　xiāngzào　toilet soap

①白　②七

7 泉　quán　spring

泉水　quánshuǐ　spring water

①白　②水

见　见字部　jiàn zì bù　The Radical of 见

象形字"见"见上册第66页。"见"做形旁的字大多与看及视觉活动有关。"见"一般在字的右边,叫做"见字边",有时也可在字的下面。

The pictographic script 见 (see page 66, Textbook I) as a radical is often related to human vision. Generally it stands on the right of a character, but sometimes it may be used at the lower part of a character.

8 观　guān　to see, view

参观　cānguān　to visit

①又　②见

9 视　　shì　to watch

电视机　diànshìjī　TV set

① 衤　② 见

1	2

10 览　　lǎn　to read, to see

阅览室　yuèlǎnshì　reading room

① ⺌　② 见

1
2

11 觉

① jiào　sleep

睡觉　shuìjiào　to sleep

② jué　to feel, sense

觉得　juéde　to feel

① ⺌　② 见

1
2

贝　　贝字旁　bèi zì páng　The Radical of 贝

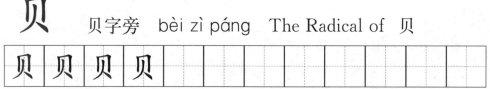

因为在中国古代贝壳曾被用做货币，所以"贝"做形旁的字常常与钱财有关。"贝"做形旁常在字的左侧或下方。

The characters with the pictophonetic 贝 as a radical are related to "currency" or "money" because in ancient times shells were used as a currency. As a radical, 贝 is often used at the left or lower part of a character.

12 贝　　bèi　shell fish

① 贝

1

13 **贵** guì noble, expensive

贵姓 guìxìng What's you name, please?

1	
2	

①虫 [口 | 中 | 虫] ②贝

14 **货** huò goods

售货员 shòuhuòyuán salesman, saleswoman

1	
2	

①化(huà) ②贝

15 **费** fèi fee, to cost

学费 xuéfèi tuition fee

生活费 shēnghuófèi living expense

1	
2	

①弗(fú) [⼀ | ⼁ | 弓 | 韦 | 弗] ②贝

16 **贸** mào trade

贸易 màoyì trade

外贸 wàimào foreign trade

1	2
3	

①⺹ [⺀ | ⺋ | ⺋] ②刀 ③贝

17 **贺** hè to congratulate

祝贺 zhùhè to congratulate

1	
2	

①加 ②贝

18 **员** yuán member

运动员 yùndòngyuán sportsman, sportswoman

1	
2	

①口 ②贝

页 页字边 yè zì biān The Radical of 页

"页"做形旁的字常与头和颈有关。页字旁一般在字的右侧。

页	页	页	页	页	页						

The characters with the pictophonetic 页 as a radical are often related to "head" or "neck". Generally it stands on the right of a character.

19 页 yè page

1

网页 wǎngyè web page
主页 zhǔyè main page
①页

20 预 yù in advance

1 2

预习 yùxí to preview
预报 yùbào forecast
①予 (yǔ) | ㇇ | ㇇ | 予 | 予 | ②页

21 颜 yán colour

1 2

颜色 yánsè colour
①彦 (yàn) | 丶 | 亠 | 亠 | 亠 | 立 | 产 | 彦 | ②页

22 题 tí to inscribe

1 2

问题 wèntí question
①是 ②页

23 顾 gù to care about

1 2

照顾 zhàogù to take care of
①厄 | 一 | 厂 | 厈 | 厄 | ②页

斤 斤字边 jīn zì biān The Radical of 斤

象形字"斤"见上册第 97 页。"斤"做形旁的字多与斧头、砍折有关。斤字旁常在字的右侧。"斤"有时也做声旁。

> The pictographic script 斤 (see page 97, Textbook I) as a radical is often related to "axe" or "chopping". Generally it stands on the right of a charcter. Sometimes 斤 may be used as a phonetic component.

㉔ 新　xīn　new

新年　xīnnián　new year
①亲　②斤

㉕ 所　suǒ　place

所以　suǒyǐ　therefore
所有　suǒyǒu　all
①斤　[´　厂　斤　斤]　②斤

㉖ 近　jìn　near

最近　zuìjìn　recent
①斤　②辶　[丶　辶　辶]

巾　巾字旁　jīn zì páng　The Radical of　巾

象形字"巾"见上册第108页。"巾"做形旁的字多与布等织物有关。巾字旁位置较灵活,可以在字的下部,也可在字的左侧或右侧,在字的左侧要写得瘦长一些。

> The pictographic script 巾 (see page 108, Textbook I) as a radical is often connected with "cloth" or anything of that kind. It may be placed on the left or right of a character, or at its lower part. When used as a left radical it should be written narrowly.

27 布　bù　cloth

布鞋　bù xié　cloth shoes

①ナ [一] [ナ] ②巾

28 币　bì　currency

人民币　rénmínbì　Renminbi

外币　wàibì　foreign currencies

①一 ②巾

29 市　shì　city, market

市长　shìzhǎng　mayor

超市　chāoshì　supermarket

①一 ②巾

30 师　shī　teacher, master

老师　lǎoshī　teacher

律师　lùshī　lawyer

①丿 [丨] [丿] ②一 ③巾

31 带　dài　to bring

带来　dàilái　to bring

①卅 [一] [十] [卅] [卅] ②宀 ③巾

32 常　cháng　often, normal

常常　chángcháng　often

①尚(shàng zì tóu) [丨] [丷] [业] [业] [严] [尚] ②巾

33 帮　bāng　to help

帮助　bāngzhù　to help

①十②邦(bāng) [一] [二] [三] [丰] [邦] [邦] ③巾

34 帽　　mào　hat

帽子　màozi　hat

| 1 | 2 |
| | 3 |

①巾　②冃 丨 冂 冂 冃　③目

认读词、词组和句子

Read the Following Words，Phrases and Sentences

一、认读词、词组

Read the Following Words and Phrases.

破：破书　破车　破衣服　破坏　打破

矿：矿山　矿泉水

号码：电话号码　房间号码　手机号码

观：参观　观看　观感　观望

视：电视　视力　近视眼　视听　轻视　远视
　　可视电话

觉：(jiào)睡一觉　睡午觉　(jué)觉得　感觉　听觉　视觉

贵：贵姓　贵国　贵客　贵公司　贵校

货：百货大楼　货物　售货员　货车

费：费用　学费　生活费　公费　自费　小费　手机费
　　房(fáng)租费　费力　费钱　费时

贸：贸易　外贸

员：售票员　售货员　人员　运动员　船员　成员
　　会员

预：预习　预报　天气预报　预先　预感

题：问题　试题　难题　考题　练习题　话题　主题

新：新年　新闻　新书　新衣服　新生

所：所以 一所学校
近：最近 近来 近视
市：市场 城市 市区 市民
师：老师 工程师 律师 师生 师姐 师妹
师兄 师弟

二、认读下列句子

Read the Following Sentences.

1. 下星期市长要去参观他们的工厂。
2. 我带一些外币去银行换人民币。
3. 我觉得那顶(dǐng)帽子的颜色不错。
4. 王老师没有睡午觉的习惯。
5. 我弟弟在大学学习贸易,在我们国家,大学的学费比较贵。
6. 我每天晚上看一会儿电视新闻,然后复习课文、预习生词、做练习题,每天差不多十一点睡觉。
7. 她以前是一个运动员,现在做贸易工作。
8. 老师,昨天你借我的磁带,我忘了带来了。
9. 你知不知道他的电话号码是多少?
10. 山本的爸爸是律师,妈妈是售货员,他自己以前是一个篮球运动员。
11. 一会儿我要去超市买一些香皂、牙膏、牙刷等日用品(basic commodities)。
12. 我刚才不小心打破了一只碗,把手也划破了。
13. 最近她妈妈住院了,她要照顾妈妈,所以请了一个星期的假。
14. 她是我的中国朋友,我学习有问题的时候,她常常帮助我。
15. 新年快到了,祝贺大家新年快乐!

第十八课

基本知识
Rudiments of Chinese Characters

查字典(二)
The Consultation of a Dictionary (B)

笔画查字法
Finding Characters by Using the Index of Stroke Numbers

音序查字法是国际通用的方法,方便、科学,但是,如果你不知道汉字的读音,就需要用其他方法了。目前普遍使用的是"笔画查字法"和"部首查字法"。

The phonetic index is an internationally-used covenient and scientific arrangement by which any word can be located in a dictionary. However it is not useful for those who do not know the pronunciation of the character that they want to look up. What are commonly-used now are indexes of stroke numbers and radicals.

笔画查字法是按照汉字笔画的多少来查字的一种方法,笔画少的在前,笔画多的在后,其步骤如下:

An index of stroke numbers is good for learners to find the character they want in an ascending order of stroke numers. The basic steps are as follows:

1. 按规范字形、笔形数数清被查字的笔画数。

Count the stroke numbers of the standardized character to be looked up.

2. 按笔画数在《笔画索引》或《笔画检字表》中找到该笔画数。

Find the stroke numbers group in the "Index of Stroke Numbers" or the "Index of Characters Grouped by Stroke Numbers".

3. 按下列起笔顺序，找到你要查的字。

Locate the character you want in the following stroke order.

①横　　一（乀　　　　　　　　　　　　　　　　）
②竖　　丨（丿　）　　　　　　　　　　　　　　　）
③撇　　丿（丿　一　　　　　　　　　　　　　　　）
④点　　丶（乀　乀　乛　　　　　　　　　　　　　）
⑤横折　フ（乛　コ　了　乛　乛　乁　乙　乚　）
⑥竖折　乚（乚　乚　乚　乁　乚　乥　　　　　）

笔画检字表中每个汉字旁边的数目表示该字在字典正文中的页码。

The number against each character in the index indicates the number of the page where the very character is to be located in the dictionary.

生字词表
List of New Characters and Words

1.	历	lì	to go through
	历史	lìshǐ	history
2.	原	yuán	original
	原来	yuánlái	original
3.	厅	tīng	hall
	客厅	kètīng	sitting room
4.	床	chuáng	bed
	起床	qǐ chuáng	to get up
5.	庆	qìng	to celebrate
	国庆节	Guóqìng Jié	National Day
6.	店	diàn	shop
	商店	shāngdiàn	shop

	饭店	fàndiàn	hotel，restaurant
	书店	shūdiàn	bookstore
7.	座	zuò	seat
	座位	zuòwèi	seat
8.	应	yīng	should
	应该	yīnggāi	should
9.	度	dù	degree
	温度	wēndù	temperature
10.	麻	má	
	麻烦	máfan	to trouble，troublous
11.	康	kāng	healthy
	健康	jiànkāng	healthy
12.	尸	shī	corpse
13.	居	jū	to live
	邻居	línjū	neighbour
14.	局	jú	bureau
	邮局	yóujú	post office
	公安局	gōng'ānjú	public security bureau
15.	展	zhǎn	to display
	展览	zhǎnlǎn	exhibition
	发展	fāzhǎn	to develop
16.	层	céng	floor
	二层楼	èr céng lóu	two-storeyed building
17.	屋	wū	house，room
	房屋	fángwū	house，buildings
18.	户	hù	door
	户口	hùkǒu	registered residence
19.	房	fáng	house
	房间	fángjiān	room
	房租	fángzū	rent
	厨房	chúfáng	kitchen
20.	动	dòng	to move
	动物	dòngwù	animal
	动物园	dòngwùyuán	zoo
	运动	yùndòng	motion，sports

21.	助	zhù	to help
	帮助	bāngzhù	to help
	自动	zìdòng	auto
	自动柜员机	zìdòng guìyuánjī	automated teller machine(ATM)
22.	加	jiā	to add
	更加	gèngjiā	more
	加油	jiāyóu	to refuel, to make more efforts
23.	努	nǔ	to make an effort
	努力	nǔlì	to work hard
24.	旗	qí	flag
	国旗	guóqí	national flag
25.	族	zú	clan
	民族	mínzú	nationality
26.	旅	lǚ	journey
	旅行	lǚxíng	to travel
	旅馆	lǚguǎn	hotel
27.	放	fàng	to put, to place
	放心	fàngxīn	to feel relieved, to set one's mind at rest
	放假	fàngjià	to have a holiday (vacation)
28.	访	fǎng	to visit
	访问	fǎngwèn	to visit
29.	欠	qiàn	to owe, yawn
30.	吹	chuī	to blow, to boast
	吹牛	chuīniú	to boast
31.	欢	huān	happy, joyful
	欢迎	huānyíng	to welcome
32.	次	cì	(a measure word)
	一次	yí cì	once
	上次	shàng cì	last time
	下次	xià cì	next time
	这次	zhè cì	this time
	每次	měi cì	every time
33.	歌	gē	song
	唱歌	chàng gē	to sing

生字的结构和书写

The Structures and Writing of the New Characters

厂　厂字头　chǎng zì tóu　The Radical of 厂

象形字"厂"见上册第 110 页。"厂"做形旁的字多与山崖或房屋有关。

The pictographic script 厂（see page 110，Textbook I）as a radical is often related to cliffs or houses.

① 历　lì　to go through

历史　lìshǐ　history
①厂　②力

② 原　yuán　original

原来　yuánlái　original
①厂　②白　③小

③ 厅　tīng　hall

客厅　kètīng　sitting room
①厂　②丁（dīng）

广　广字头　guǎng zì tóu　The Radical of 广

象形字"广"见上册第 111 页。"广"做形旁的字多与房屋有关。

The pictographic script 广（see page 111，Textbook I）as a radical is often related to houses.

4 床 chuáng bed

起床 qǐ chuáng to get up
①广 ②木

5 庆 qìng to celebrate

国庆节 Guóqìng Jié National Day
①广 ②大

6 店 diàn shop

商店 shāngdiàn shop
饭店 fàndiàn hotel, restaurant
书店 shūdiàn bookstore
①广 ②占（zhàn）

7 座 zuò seat

座位 zuòwèi seat
①广 ②坐

8 应 yīng should

应该 yīnggāi should
①广 ②⺍ 丶 丶 ⺍ ⺌

9 度 dù degree

温度 wēndù temperature
①广 ②廿 ③又

10 麻 má

麻烦 máfan to trouble, troublous
①广 ②＋③林

11 康　kāng　healthy

健康　jiànkāng　healthy

①广　②隶(lì)　｜ㄱ｜ㄱ｜ㅋ｜尹｜尹｜尹｜隶

尸字头　sī zì tóu　The Radical of 尸

12 尸　shī　corpse

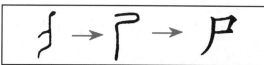

古字像一个身体挺直、侧坐着的人。这是古代祭祀时,代替死者受祭的人。

The ancient written form of 尸 is like a side view of a man sitting up. In the olden days a man was supposed to receive the sacrificial offerings for the dead in a memorial ceremony.

尸　尸　尸

第三笔"竖撇"与第一、二笔相接。

The third stroke of 尸 is connected with its first and second strokes.

"尸"做形旁的字一般与身体及人体活动有关。

The pictographic script 尸 as a radical is often related to human body or physical movement.

13 居　jū　to live

邻居　línjū　neighbour

①尸　②古(gǔ)　一｜十｜古

14 局　jú　bureau

邮局　yóujú　post office

公安局　gōng'ānjú　public security bureau

①尸　②司

15 展　zhǎn　to display

展览　zhǎnlǎn　exhibition

发展　fāzhǎn　to develop

①尸　②共　③K

16 层　céng　floor

二层楼　èr céng lóu　two-storeyed building

①尸　②云

17 屋　wū　house, room

房屋　fángwū　house, buildings

①尸　②至

户　户字头　hù zì tóu　The Radical of　户

18 户　hù　door

户口　hùkǒu　registered residence

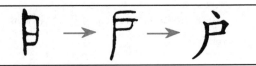

古字像一扇门的样子。

The ancient written form of 户 is in the shape of a door.

户 户 户 户

"尸"字上面加一"点"。

户 can be written by adding a dot to 尸 on the top.

"户"做形旁的字多与门或人家有关。

The pictographic script 户 as a radical is generally related to "door" or "household".

19 房 fáng house

房间 fángjiān room
房租 fángzū rent
厨房 chúfáng kitchen
①户 ②方

力 力字旁 lì zì páng The Radical of 力

象形字"力"见上册第105页。"力"做形旁的字大多与力气或劳动有关。力字旁的位置比较灵活。

The pictographic script 力 (see page 105, Textbook I) as a radical is often related to "strength" or "labour". It can be used on different sides of a character.

20 动 dòng to move

动物 dòngwù animal
动物园 dòngwùyuán zoo
运动 yùndòng motion, sports
自动 zìdòng auto
自动柜员机 zìdòng guìyuánjī automated teller machine (ATM)
①云 ②力

21 助 zhù to help

帮助 bāngzhù to help
①且 ②力

22 加　jiā　to add

|1|2|

更加　gèngjiā　more
加油　jiāyóu　to refuel，to make more efforts
①力　　②口

23 努　nǔ　to make an effort

|1|2|
|3| |

努力　nǔlì　to work hard
①＋②奴(nú)　| 女 | 奴 |　　③力

方　　方字旁　fāng zì páng　The Radical of 方

"方"做形旁的字多与旗子有关。方字旁常在字的左侧。

> The characters with the pictophonetic 方 as a left radical of a character are often related to flags or things of that type.

| 方 | 方 | 方 | 方 | | | | | | | | | |

24 旗　qí　flag

|1|2|
| |3|

国旗　guóqí　national flag
①方　　②⼂　　③其(qí)

25 族　zú　clan

|1|2|
| |3|

民族　mínzú　nation ality
①方　　②⼂　　③矢

26 旅　lǚ　journey

|1|2|
| |3|

旅行　lǚxíng　to travel
旅馆　lǚguǎn　hotel
①方　　②⼂　　③氏　| ⼂ | ⼁ | ⼂ | 氏 |

27 放　fàng　to put，to place

放心　fàngxīn　to feel relieved，to set one's mind at rest
放假　fàngjià　to have a hoilday vacation

| 1 | 2 |

①方　②攵　丿　丆　ケ　攵

28 访　fǎng　to visit

访问　fǎngwèn　to visit

| 1 | 2 |

①讠　②方

欠　欠字旁　qiàn zì páng　The Radical of 欠

29 欠　qiàn　to owe，yawn

古字像一个跪坐着的人仰头张嘴大打呵欠的样子。本义是指"张口出气"，即打呵欠。后借用为"欠债"的"欠"。

The ancient written form of 欠 is like a man on knees, looking up and yawning. The character originally meant "yawn", but now has by extension come to mean "owe somebody something".

| 欠 | 欠 | 欠 | 欠 | | | | | | | | |

第二笔"横钩"与第一笔"撇"相接，下面是"人"。

The second stroke of 欠 is a horizontal hook, touching the left-falling stroke. Underneath is the component 人.

　　"欠"做形旁的字多与张嘴呵气及神情心意的表达有关,欠字旁在字的右侧。

The characters with the pictophonetic 欠 as a right radical are often associated with breathing out or a mental expression.

30 吹　　chuī　to blow, to boast

吹牛　chuīniú　to boast

| 1 | 2 |

①口　②欠

31 欢　　huān　happy, joyful

欢迎　huānyíng　to welcome

| 1 | 2 |

①又 [又 丁] [又]　②欠

32 次　　cì　(a measure word)

一次　yí cì　once

上次　shàng cì　last time

下次　xià cì　next time

这次　zhè cì　this time

每次　měi cì　every time

| 1 | 2 |

①冫 [丶] [冫]　②欠

33 歌　　gē　song

唱歌　chàng gē　to sing

| 1 | 2 |

①哥(gē)　②欠

认读词、词组和句子

Read the Following Words，Phrases and Sentences

一、认读词、词组

Read the Following Words and Phrases.

厅：客厅　大厅　餐厅　舞厅　候机厅　音乐厅　休息厅

庆：庆祝　欢庆　国庆节

店：商店　饭店　书店　酒店　鞋店　水果店　咖啡店

座：让座　一座山　一座楼

度：温度　长度　高度　难度

居：邻居　居民　居住　旧居　新居

展览：展览馆　展览会　展览品　展览大厅

屋：屋子　屋里　屋外　书屋

户：户口　窗户　用户　住户

房：房子　楼房　书房　房东　新房

动：动作　动词　感动　自动

加：加班　加快　加热　加入　参加

旅：旅行　旅游　旅馆　旅客

放：放心　放学　放大　放假

欢：喜欢　欢乐　欢庆　欢迎

次：一次　上次　下次　每次　有次　多次　这次　那次　哪次　首次　第一次

歌：唱歌　一首歌　中文歌　外文歌　歌手　歌星　歌词　国歌　民歌　儿歌　情歌

二、认读下列句子

Read the Following Sentences.

1. 他先去邮局,然后去商店;我去展销馆看展览。

2. 他原来学习历史专业,后来觉得没意思,就换成经贸专业了。

3. 你们国家的国庆节是几月几号? 中国的国庆节是十月一号,全国放假三天。

4. 我们是邻居,应该互相帮助,互相照顾。

5. 中国有五十六个民族,汉族人口最多。

6. 欢迎麦克再唱一首中文歌。

7. 这学期他学习更加努力了。

8. 我们的首相(prime minister)来中国访问了,今天下午我们国家的留学生都去大使馆。

9. 你放心吧,要是有问题,他会帮助你的。

10. 明天的最高温度是零下五度。

11. 中国的经济(jīngjì, economy)正在健康地发展。

12. 运动场上,大家都在为长跑运动员加油。

13. 报纸上有很多房屋出租广告,但是房租都太贵了。

14. 那套(tào)房子不错,在十层,有厨房、客厅、卫生间(wèishēngjiān, toilet),两个房间也都很大。

15. 我昨天刚从南方旅行回来,睡得很晚,所以今天上午十点才起床。

16. A:每次到北京,都要麻烦你。

   B:我们是好朋友,这是应该的。

第十九课

基本知识
Rudiments of Chinese Characters

查字典(三)
The Consultation of a Dictionary (C)

部首查字法
Finding Characters by Using an Index of Radicals

　　部首查字法是根据汉字的部首来查字的一种方法。把某一个相同部件的汉字编成一组,用这个相同的部件作为这一组的标记,叫做"部首"。部首以及同一部首内的字按笔画数从少到多排列。部首查字法的步骤如下:

An index of radicals is useful for learners to locate a character in the dictionary. Radicals are common markers by which characters that have similar side components are grouped together. Radicals and the characters under each of them are arranged in an ascending order of stroke numbers. An index of characters can be used by following the steps below:

1. 找出部首

Decide the right radical that the character to be looked up.

2. 数部首笔画

Count the stroke numbers of the radical

3. 在《部首目录》中找到该部首的页码

Find out the page number of the radical in the "Catalogue of Radicals".

4. 根据上述页码在《检字表》中找到该部首

Open the dictionary to the page and locate the character in the "Index of the Characters".

5. 数该汉字除部首以外部分的笔画数

Count the total stroke numbers of the character apart from that of the radical.

6. 找到该字在字典或词典正文中的页码

Find out the page number of the character in the dictionary.

7. 根据上述页码在正文中找到该字

Look up the character on the page indicated.

部首查字法的关键在于确定部首。如果一个合体字的几个部件都是部首,一般只取其中的一个作为该字的部首。确定的原则是:

The decision of a radical is very important in locating a character by using an index of radicals. When there are more than two components that can all be radicals in a combined character, only one of them functions as its radical. The following are essential points for deciding a radical:

1. 上下结构,取上不取下。如:志(取士部)、采(取⺥部)。

The upper component is the radical of the character in upper-and-lower formation, e. g. 志 and 采.

2. 左右结构,取左不取右。如:相(取木部)、利(取禾部)。

The left component is the radical of the character in left-and-right formation, e. g. 相 and 利.

3. 内外结构,取外不取内。如:闻(取门部)、句(取勹部)。

The outer part is the radical of the character in outside-and-inside formation, e. g. 闻 and 句.

有的字典或词典为了查检方便,把同一个字列入不同的部首中。如 "相",在木部和目部都可以查到。

Some of the characters may be listed in different radical groups for convenience. For instance, 相 is included under both 木 and 目.

有的独体字没有可以做部首的偏旁,就可以查中坐。如:半(丨部)、世(一部)、办(力部);没有中坐的,可以查字的左上角。如:为(丶部)、些(止部);如果实在无法查时,可以查一般字典或词典都有的《难检字笔画索引》或《难字表》,表中的汉字是按全字的笔画多少排列的。

If a single character contains no side component that can be used as a radical, its central part may be considered the grouping stroke that it is listed under, e. g. the vertical of 半, the horizontal of 世, the 力 of 办. If such a character has no central part its top left stroke may be used as the grouping indicator, e. g. the、of 为, the 止 of 些. Supposing no stroke of a character is useful for the decision of its location in the dictionary, one can always make good use of "The Stroke Index of Complicated Characters" or "The Index of Complicated Characters" in which all characters are arranged in an order of stroke numbers.

生字词表

List of New Characters and Words

1.	弓	gōng	bow
2.	张	zhāng	(a measure word), to open
	紧张	jǐnzhāng	tense
3.	弯	wān	to curve
	拐弯	guǎi wān	to turn to

4.	鸡	jī	chicken
	鸡蛋	jīdàn	egg
	鸡肉	jīròu	chicken
5.	鸭	yā	duck
	烤鸭	kǎoyā	roast duck
6.	鹅	é	goose
	天鹅	tiān'é	swan
7.	翻	fān	to turn over，to translate
	翻译	fānyì	to translate，to interpret
8.	扇	shàn	fan
	电风扇	diànfēngshàn	electric fan
9.	酉	yǒu	tenth of the twelve Earthly Branches
10.	醒	xǐng	to wake up
11.	醉	zuì	drunk
	喝醉	hēzuì	drunk
12.	酸	suān	sour
	酸奶	suānnǎi	yoghurt
13.	界	jiè	circle
	世界	shìjiè	world
14.	画	huà	painting，to draw
	画儿	huàr	paintings，drawing
	画报	huàbào	pictorial
15.	留	liú	to stay, to leave
	留学	liúxué	to study abroad
	留学生	liúxuéshēng	foreign student
16.	累	lèi	tired
	累死了	lèisǐ le	dog-tired
17.	皿	mǐn	household utensils
18.	盘	pán	dish
	盘子	pánzi	tray
	光盘	guāngpán	CD
19.	盒	hé	box
	盒子	hézi	box

20. 士	shì	scholar, person trained in a specified field
护士	hùshi	nurse
博士	bóshì	doctor
21. 志	zhì	will
同志	tóngzhì	comrade
22. 声	shēng	sound
声音	shēngyīn	sound
声调	shēngdiào	tone
23. 喜	xǐ	happy
喜欢	xǐhuan	to like
24. 问	wèn	to ask
请问	qǐngwèn	I should like to ask
25. 间	jiān	(a measure word), room, between
卫生间	wèishēngjiān	toilet
中间	zhōngjiān	among, centre, middle
26. 阅	yuè	to read
阅读	yuèdú	to read
27. 闹	nào	noisy
热闹	rènao	busy
闹钟	nàozhōng	alarm clock
28. 分	fēn	to divide, minute
分钟	fēnzhōng	minute
分开	fēnkāi	to separate
十分	shífēn	very
29. 半	bàn	half
一半	yíbàn	an half
30. 单	dān	single, bill, list
简单	jiǎndān	simple
买单	mǎi dān	to pay a bill

31. 只	①zhī	(a measure word)
一只鸭	yì zhī yā	a duck
	②zhǐ	only
只好	zhǐhǎo	have to
32. 真	zhēn	true, really, indeed
真正	zhēnzhèng	genuine, true
33. 其	qí	its
其他	qítā	rest

生字的结构和书写

The Structures and Writing of the New Characters

弓　　弓字旁　gōng zì páng　The Radical 弓

① 弓　gōng　bow

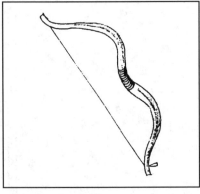

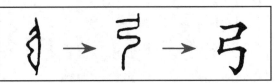

古字像一把弓的形状。

The ancient written form of 弓 is like a bow.

弓 弓 弓

"弓"做形旁的字一般与弓有关。弓字旁常在字的左侧，有时也可在下边。

The characters with the pictophonetic 弓 as a radical are generally related to a bow. It often stands on the left of a character, sometimes it can be used at its lower part.

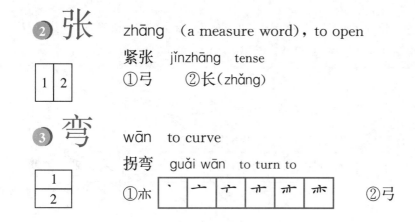

② 张   zhāng   (a measure word)，to open

紧张   jǐnzhāng   tense

①弓   ②长(zhǎng)

③ 弯   wān   to curve

拐弯   guǎi wān   to turn to

①亦   丶 亠 亠 办 亦 亦   ②弓

鸟   鸟字旁 niǎo zì páng   The Radical of 鸟

象形字"鸟"见上册第 90 页。"鸟"做形旁的字多与鸟类有关。鸟字旁常在字的右侧。

The pictographic script 鸟 (see page 90, Textbook I) as a right radical is often related to birds.

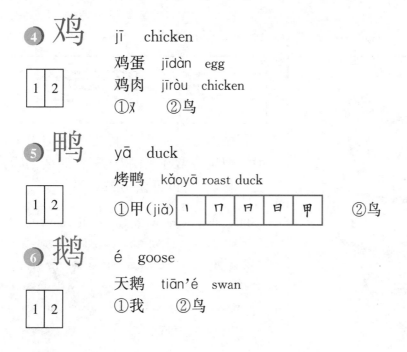

④ 鸡   jī   chicken

鸡蛋   jīdàn   egg
鸡肉   jīròu   chicken
①又   ②鸟

⑤ 鸭   yā   duck

烤鸭   kǎoyā   roast duck

①甲(jiǎ)   丨 冂 日 日 甲   ②鸟

⑥ 鹅   é   goose

天鹅   tiān'é   swan

①我   ②鸟

羽   羽字旁   yǔ zì páng   The Radical of 羽

象形字"羽"见上册第 92 页，"羽"做形旁的字多与羽毛有关，羽字旁位置比较灵活。

The pictographic script 羽 (see page 92, Textbook I) as a radical is often related to "feather". It may stand on different sides of a character.

7 翻   fān   to turn over，to translate

翻译   fānyì   to translate，to interpret

1	3
2	

①＋②番（fān）｜ 一 ｜ 丆 ｜ 亚 ｜ 平 ｜ 釆 ｜ 采 ｜ 番 ｜ ③羽

8 扇   shàn   fan

电风扇   diànfēngshàn   electric fan

1	
	2

①户   ②羽

酉   酉字旁   yǒu zì páng   The Radical of 酉

9 酉   yǒu   tenth of the twelve Earthly Branches

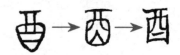

"酉"做形旁的字多与酒及化学类事物有关。酉字旁常在字的左侧，这时要写得瘦长一些，有时也可在字的下部。

The characters with the pictophonetic 酉 as a radical are often related to "wine" or anything chemical. When standing on the left of a character it should be written narrowly. It may also be used at the lower part of a character.

酉 酉 酉 酉 酉 酉 酉

第五笔"竖弯"，不带钩。字形较长。

The fifth stroke of 酉 is a vertical turning without a hook. The character is narrow-sized.

⑩ 醒 xǐng to wake up

①酉 ②星（xīng）

⑪ 醉 zuì drunk

喝醉 hēzuì drunk

①酉 ②卒（zú）

⑫ 酸 suān sour

酸奶 suānnǎi yoghurt

①酉 ②夋

田 田字旁 tián zì páng The Radical of 田

象形字"田"见上册第 77 页。"田"做形旁的字常与田地及农务有关。田字旁位置比较灵活。

The pictographic script 田（see page 77, Textbook I）as a radical is often related to farmland or farming. It can be used on different sides of a character.

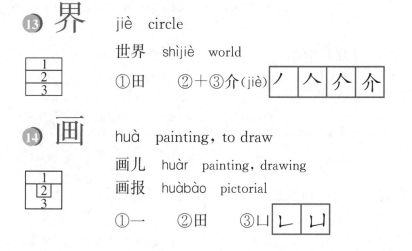

⑬ 界 jiè circle

世界 shìjiè world

①田 ②+③介（jiè）

⑭ 画 huà painting, to draw

画儿 huàr painting, drawing

画报 huàbào pictorial

①一 ②田 ③凵

15 留　liú　to stay，to leave

留学　liúxué　to study abroad
留学生　liúxuéshēng　foreign student
①卯　　②田

1
2

16 累　lèi　tired

累死了　lèisǐ le　dog-tired
①田　　②糸(mì)

1
2

皿　皿字底　mǐn zì dǐ　The Radical of 皿

17 皿　mǐn　household utensils

古字像一种带圈足的圆口容器。"皿"的本义是装东西的器具，是碗盘一类的饮食用具的总称。

The ancient written form of 皿 is in the shape of a container with a round opening and a round leg. Its original meaning is "food container" or "household utensils".

里边是两竖。注意与"四"的区别。

There are two vertical strokes inside 皿. Be aware of the difference between 皿 and 四.

"皿"做形旁的字多与盛物器皿有关，皿字底在字的下部。

The characters with the pictophonetic 皿 as a radical are often related to a kitchen container. It is generally used at the bottom of a character.

⑱ 盘 pán dish

1
2

盘子 pánzi tray
光盘 guāngpán CD
①舟 ②皿

⑲ 盒 hé box

1
2

盒子 hézi box
①合(hé) ②皿

士 士字头 shì zì tóu The Radical of 士

"士"做偏旁都在字的上部,意义不明。

The radical 士 with uncertain meaning is often used at the top of a character.

⑳ 士 shì scholar, person trained in a specified field

1

护士 hùshi nurse
博士 bóshì doctor

①士 | 一 | 十 | 士 |(注意与"土"的区别)

㉑ 志 zhì will

1
2

同志 tóngzhì comrade
①士 ②心

㉒ 声 shēng sound

1
2

声音 shēngyīn sound
声调 shēngdiào tone

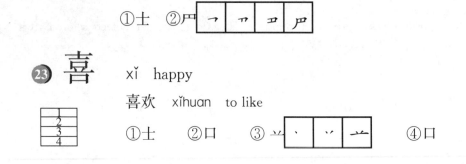

①士　②尸　㇆　㇆　㇆　尸

23 喜　　xǐ　happy

喜欢　xǐhuan　to like

①士　　②口　　③ 丷　丶　丷　丷　　④口

门　　门字框　mén zì kuàng　The Radical of 门

象形字"门"见上册第 53 页。"门"做形旁的字多与门有关。"门"有时也做声旁，如"问""们""闻"等。

> The pictographic script 门 (see page 53, Textbook I) as a radical is often related to a door.

24 问　　wèn　to ask

请问　qǐngwèn　I should like to ask

①门　　②口

25 间　　jiān　(a measure word), room, between

卫生间　wèishēngjiān　toilet

中间　zhōngjiān　among, centre, middle

①门　　②日

26 阅　　yuè　to read

阅读　yuèdú　to read

①门　　②兑

27 闹　　nào　noisy

热闹　rènao　busy

闹钟　nàozhōng　alarm clock

①门　　②市

八   八字旁   bā zì páng   The Radical of 八

"八"的本义是"分开",所以"八"做形旁的字一般与分开相背的意义有关。"八"做偏旁位置比较灵活,在字的下方时,"八"的捺笔变为长点,如"共"等。八字旁在字的上部,有时也写做"丷",如"前、首"等。

Therefore the original meaning of 八 is "separation". When used as a pictographic radical it is related to "separation" or "going in an opposite direction". It may stand on different sides of a character.

28 分   fēn   to divide, minute

1
2

分钟   fēnzhōng   minute
分开   fēnkāi   to separate
十分   shífēn   very
①八   ②刀

29 半   bàn   half

1

一半   yíbàn   an half
①半 | 丶 | 丷 | 丷 | 丷 | 半 | (注意与"羊"的区别)

30 单   dān   single, bill, list

1
2
3

简单   jiǎndān   simple
买单   mǎi dān   to pay a bill
①丷   ②日   ③十

31 只   ①zhī   (a measure word)

1
2

    一只鸭   yì zhī yā   a duck
②zhǐ   only
    只好   zhǐhǎo   have to
①口   ②八

32 真

zhēn　true，really，indeed

真正　zhēnzhèng　genuine，true

1
2
3

①一　②且 | 冂 冃 月 目 且（注意与"且"的区别）　③八

33 其

qí　its

其他　qítā　rest

1
2

①其 一 十 艹 丗 甘 其　②八

认读词、词组和句子

Read the Following Words，Phrases and Sentences

一、认读词、词组
Read the Following Words and Phrases.

张：一张报纸　一张床　一张桌子　一张弓　紧张
张开

鸡：鸡蛋　小鸡　母鸡　公鸡　鸡肉　火鸡　鸡丁

画：画报　画儿　画家　画展　国画　名画　动画片

声：声音　大声　小声　高声　声母　声调(diào)　歌声
钟声

问：请问　问题　问候　问好　问答　问号　访问　学问

间：房间　时间　卫生间　中间　早间　午间　一间屋子

分：十分钟　分机　分店　分公司　分开　分手　学分
十分

半：半天　半年　半个月　半斤　半小时　半票　一半
一大半　北半球　南半球　东半球　西半球

单:简单 单一 单人床 单身汉 单相思 菜单
　　床单 名单

只:(zhī) 一只老虎 一只眼睛 一只鸟 一只鸡
　　　　一只鸭 一只鹅 一只鞋 一只脚
　　(zhǐ) 只是 只有 只要 只顾

真:真人 真心 真话 真是 真情 真假 认真

二、认读下列句子
Read the Following Sentences.

1. 我房间的电风扇不知道为什么坏了。

2. 他去美国留学了,在那儿读完博士才回来。

3. 昨天买的闹钟在那个盒子里,还没拿出来呢。

4. 这个句子十分简单,大家都翻译对了。

5. 你饿了吗? 盘子里有两个鸡蛋,你吃了吧,桌子上还有酸奶。

6. 你喜欢吃北京烤鸭吗?

7. 对不起,我忘了打电话了。昨天晚上喝醉了,今天上午八点四十五分才醒。

8. 我们在上阅读课,请外面的同学说话声音小点儿。

9. 今天很多同学在阿里的房间祝贺他的生日,他们又唱歌又跳舞,真热闹。

10. 我去云南少数(shǎoshù)民族地区旅行了,刚回来,累死了。

11. 上次口语考试的时候,我太紧张了,很多简单的句子都没听懂,只好请老师再说一遍(biàn)。

12. 同志,请问你这儿有没有《中国画报》?

13. 真正的朋友是在你有困难的时候,热情帮助你的人。

14. 我昨天晚上看了一场芭蕾(bālěi)舞(ballet)《天鹅湖(hú, lake)》,四小天鹅跳得真美,其他的人跳得也不错。

15. A:请问,卫生间在哪儿?

　　B:前面向右拐弯,走到头。

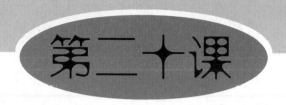

LESSON

基本知识

Rudiments of Chinese Characters

汉字的偏旁（五）

The Radicals of Chinese Characters（E）

一些汉字的形符对汉字意义的类属有一定的提示作用。在这些形符中，有些是成字形符，它们是由已经学过的象形字来充当的，如：口、日、木、目、巾等。还有一些是不成字形符，其中有的是象形字的变体，它们是由独体字演变而来的，如"讠、亻、钅、⺮"等。还有一些形符虽然不成字，但也还是有意义的，如"冫"，它的原意是指冰破裂后的纹路，因为结冰时天气寒冷，所以用"冫"做形符的字，常常跟冷的意思有关。这样具有意义的不成字形符，还有"氵、宀、艹、疒"等。

Some pictographic elements can act as hints for the categories of characters' meanings. Among these pictographic elements, some are well-developed characters, which are pictographs, such as 口、木、目 and 巾. Others are under-developed characters, some of which are pictographs' transformations derived form single characters, such as the radicals 讠、亻、钅 and ⺮. And there exist some pictographic elements which are not characters but have certain meanings, e. g. 冫, whose original meaning was "the lines of the broken ice". When water water is frozen, it is very cold. So the characters with 冫 as the pictographic element are related to "coldness". Such pictographic elements include 氵、宀、艹、疒, etc.

生字词表
List of New Characters and Words

1.	冷	lěng	cold
	寒冷	hánlěng	cold，icy
2.	凉	liáng	cool，cold
	凉快	liángkuai	nice and cool
3.	净	jìng	clean
	干净	gānjìng	clean
4.	准	zhǔn	precise，to allow
	准备	zhǔnbèi	to prepare，to plan
5.	决	jué	to decide，absolutely
	决定	juédìng	to decide，decision
6.	况	kuàng	circumstance，moveover
	情况	qíngkuàng	circumstance
7.	冬	dōng	winter
	冬天	dōngtiān	winter
8.	寒	hán	cold
	寒假	hánjià	winter vacation
9.	江	jiāng	river
	长江	Cháng Jiāng	the Changjiang（Yangtze）River
10.	河	hé	river
	黄河	Huáng Hé	the Yellow River
11.	湖	hú	lake
	西湖	Xīhú	West Lake
12.	海	hǎi	sea
	大海	dàhǎi	sea
	上海	Shànghǎi	Shanghai
13.	洗	xǐ	to wash
	洗衣机	xǐyījī	washing machine

14. 澡	zǎo	bath
洗澡	xǐzǎo	to take a bath
15. 漂	piào	
漂亮	piàoliang	pretty，beautiful
16. 注	zhù	note
注意	zhùyì	to pay attention to
17. 清	qīng	clear
清楚	qīngchu	clear
18. 满	mǎn	full
满意	mǎnyì	satisfied
不满	bùmǎn	dissatisfied
19. 法	fǎ	law，method
语法	yǔfǎ	grammar
法语	Fǎyǔ	French
法律	fǎlǜ	law
办法	bànfǎ	way
方法	fāngfǎ	method，way
20. 演	yǎn	to perform
演出	yǎnchū	to perform，show
表演	biǎoyǎn	to perform
开演	kāiyǎn	to begin a performance
21. 游	yóu	to swim
游览	yóulǎn	to go sightseeing
22. 泳	yǒng	to swim
游泳	yóuyǒng	to swim
23. 家	jiā	family, home, specialist in a certain field
大家	dàjiā	everybody
画家	huàjiā	painter
家具	jiājù	furniture
24. 宿	sù	to stay overnight
宿舍	sùshè	dormitory
25. 字	zì	character
汉字	hànzì	Chinese character
生字	shēngzì	new word

26. 安	ān	safe
安全	ānquán	safety
晚安	wǎn'ān	good night
27. 完	wán	to finish
完成	wánchéng	to finish
28. 定	dìng	surely, to decide, to fix
一定	yídìng	surely
不一定	bù yídìng	not sure, may not
29. 宜	yí	suitable
便宜	piányi	cheap
30. 赛	sài	to compete
比赛	bǐsài	to compete
31. 冠	guàn	crown
冠军	guànjūn	champion
32. 军	jūn	army
军人	jūnrén	armyman
33. 写	xiě	to write
听写	tīngxiě	dictation
34. 茶	chá	tea
绿茶	lùchá	green tea
红茶	hóngchá	black tea
茶馆	cháguǎn	teahouse
茶叶	cháyè	tea, tea leaves
花茶	huāchá	scented tea
35. 苹	píng	
苹果	píngguǒ	apple
36. 花	huā	flower, to spend
花园	huāyuán	garden
开花	kāi huā	to bloom
花钱	huā qián	to spend money
37. 英	yīng	England
英语	Yīngyǔ	English
38. 草	cǎo	grass
草地	cǎodì	grassland, lawn

39.	黄	huáng	yellow
	黄瓜	huángguā	cucumber
	黄色	huángsè	yellow
40.	蕉	jiāo	any of several broadleaf plants
	香蕉	xiāngjiāo	banana

生字的结构和书写
The Structures and Writing of the New Characters

冫　两点水儿　liǎng diǎn shuǐr　　The Radical of 冫

古字形像冰块破裂后的纹路。"冫"做形旁的字多和寒冷的意思有关。两点水一般在左侧。

The radical was originally in the shape of the lines on broken ice. Therefore it is related to "cold". It often stands on the left of a character.

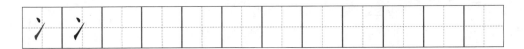

① 冷　lěng　cold

寒冷　hánlěng　cold, icy

1	2

① 冫　② 令 (lìng)

ノ	人	人	今	令

2 凉　liáng　cool, cold

1	2

凉快　liángkuai　nice and cool
① 冫　② 京

3 净　jìng　clean

1	2

干净　gānjìng　clean

① 冫　② 争 (zhēng)

′	′	今	今	今	争

4 准　zhǔn　precise, to allow

1	2

准备　zhǔnbèi　to prepare, to plan
① 冫　② 隹

5 决　jué　to decide, absolutely

1	2

决定　juédìng　to decide, decision
① 冫　② 夬

6 况　kuàng　circumstance, moreover

1	2

情况　qíngkuàng　circumstance

① 冫　② 兄

口	兄

7 冬　dōng　winter

1
2

冬天　dōngtiān　winter

① 夂

′	夕	夂

② ⼎

、	冫

8 寒　hán　cold

2
3
4

寒假　hánjià　winter vacation

① 宀　② 卅

一	二	𦍌	卅	𡉏

③ 八　④ 冫

氵 三点水儿　shān diǎn shuǐr　The Radical of 氵

古字形像水流的形状。"氵"做形旁的字大多和水或液体有关。三点水儿在字的左侧。

Originally the radical was in the shape of running water. Standing on the left of a character, it is related to "water" or "liquid".

氵	氵	氵								

9 江　jiāng　river

长江　Cháng Jiāng　the Changjiang (Yangtze) River

1	2

①氵　②工

10 河　hé　river

黄河　Huáng Hé　the Yellow River

1	2

①氵　②可

11 湖　hú　lake

西湖　Xīhú　West Lake

1	2	3

①氵　②+③胡(hú)

十	古	胡

12 海　hǎi　sea

大海　dàhǎi　sea

上海　Shànghǎi　Shanghai

1	2

①氵　②每

13 洗   xǐ   to wash

1	2

洗衣机   xǐyījī   washing machine
①氵   ②先

14 澡   zǎo   bath

1	2

洗澡   xǐzǎo   to take a bath
①氵   ②枲

15 漂   piào

1	2

漂亮   piàoliang   pretty, beautiful
①氵   ②票(piào)

16 注   zhù   note

1	2

注意   zhùyì   to pay attention to
①氵   ②主

17 清   qīng   clear

1	2

清楚   qīngchu   clear
①氵   ②青

18 满   mǎn   full

1	2
	3

满意   mǎnyì   satisfied
不满   bùmǎn   dissatisfied
①氵   ②艹 | 一 | 一 | 艹 | ③两

19 法   fǎ   law，method

1	2

语法   yǔfǎ   grammar
法语   Fǎyǔ   French
法律   fǎlǜ   law
办法   bànfǎ   way

方法　fāngfǎ　method, way
①氵　②去

⑳ 演　yǎn　to perform

1	2
	3

演出　yǎnchū　to perform, show
表演　biǎoyǎn　to perform
开演　kāiyǎn　to begin a performance

①氵　②＋③寅(yín) | 宀 | 宀 | 宁 | 官 | 宫 | 宙 | 宙 | 寅 | 寅 |

㉑ 游　yóu　to swim

1	2	3
		4

游览　yóulǎn　to go sightseeing
①氵　②方　③⺊　④子

㉒ 泳　yǒng　to swim

1	2

游泳　yóuyǒng　to swim
①氵　②永(yǒng) | 丶 | 汀 | 永 | 永 | 永 |

宀　宝盖头　bǎo gài tóu　The Radical of 宀

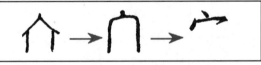

古字像房屋的形状，上面像屋顶，旁边像墙壁。"宀"做形旁的字大多和房屋有关，宝盖头总在字的上部。

The ancient written form of this radical is in the shape of a roof and of the walls on both sides. When used on the top of a character it is often related to "houses".

宀	宀	宀										

23 家 jiā family，home，specialist in a certain field

大家 dàjiā everybody
画家 huàjiā painter
家具 jiājù furniture
①宀 ②豕 一 一 丁 豕 豕 豕 豕

24 宿 sù to stay overnight

宿舍 sùshè dormitory
①宀 ②亻 ③百

25 字 zì character

汉字 hànzì Chinese character
生字 shēngzì new word
①宀 ②子

26 安 ān safe

安全 ānquán safety
晚安 wǎn'ān good night
①宀 ②女

27 完 wán to finish

完成 wánchéng to finish
①宀 ②元

28 定 dìng surely，to decide，to fix

一定 yídìng surely
不一定 bù yídìng not sure, may not
①宀 ②疋 一 丁 疋 疋 疋

29 宜 yí suitable

便宜 piányi cheap
①宀 ②且

30 赛 sài to compete

比赛 bǐsài to compete
①宀 ②龶 ③八 ④贝

秃宝盖 tū bǎo gài The Radical of 冖

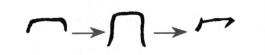

古字像以物覆盖。"冖"做形旁的字一般与覆盖的意思有关。秃宝盖在字的上部。

The ancient written form of the radical is in the shape of a cover. As a radical on the top of a character it is always related to "cover".

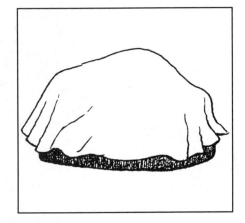

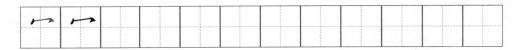

31 冠 guàn crown

冠军 guànjūn champion
①冖 ②元 ③寸

32 军 jūn army

军人 jūnrén armyman
①冖 ②车

③③ 写　xiě　to write

1
2

听写　tīngxiě　dictation

①㇆　②与(yǔ)

一	与	与

⺾　草字头　cǎo zì tóu　The Radical of ⺾

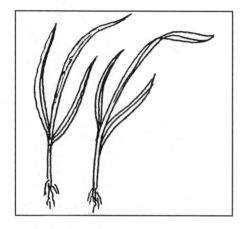

古字像两棵草的形状。"⺾"做形旁的字一般与草本植物有关。草字头在字的上部。

The ancient written form of the radical is in the double shape of grass. As a radical used on the top of a character it is often related to herbal plants.

⺾	⺾	⺾										

③④ 茶　chá　tea

1
2
3

绿茶　lǜchá　green tea
红茶　hóngchá　black tea
茶馆　cháguǎn　teahouse
茶叶　cháyè　tea, tea leaves
花茶　huāchá　scented tea

①⺾　②人　③木

③⑤ 苹　píng

1
2

苹果　píngguǒ　apple

①⺾　②平(píng)

一	丷	口	立	平

36 花

1
2

huā flower，to spend

花钱 huā qián to spend money
花园 huāyuán garden
开花 kāi huā to bloom
① 艹 ②化

37 英

1
2

yīng England

英语 Yīngyǔ English
① 艹 ②央(yāng) 丶 冂 叿 央 央

38 草

1
2

cǎo grass

草地 cǎodì grlassland，lawn
① 艹 ②早

39 黄

1
2

huáng yellow

黄瓜 huángguā cucumber
黄色 huángsè yellow
① 艹 ②更

40 蕉

2
3

jiāo any of several broadleaf plants

香蕉 xiāngjiāo banana
① 艹 ②＋③焦(jiāo) 隹 焦

认读词、词组和句子
Read the Following Words，Phrases and Sentences

一、认读词、词组
Read the Following Words and Phrases.

冷：冷饮　冷水　冷气　冷风　冷库

凉：凉快　凉水　凉鞋　凉菜　着凉

冬：冬天　冬季　寒冬　冬衣　冬瓜

寒：寒假　寒冷　寒风　寒气　寒心

江：长江　一条江　江水　江里　江面　江边　江西

河：河水　河里　河面　河北　河南　河边

湖：湖水　湖面　湖北　湖南　太湖　五湖四海

海：大海　上海　海水　海面　海军　海关　海外
　　航海　人海　下海

洗：洗衣服　洗脸　洗手　洗衣机　洗热水澡　洗碗
　　洗发水　洗面奶　洗手间

满：满意　不满　坐满了　放满

法：法语　法文　法国　语法　办法　想法　看法
　　用法　书法

演：演出　演员　开演　演说　表演

游：旅游　游人　春游　游客　游船　郊游　上游
　　中游　下游

家：大家　作家　歌唱家　专家　画家　家家户户
　　家具　家族　国家

泳：游泳　冬泳　泳衣　泳帽　游泳池(chí)

字：名字　生字　字典　字母　文字　字体　打字
　　错别字　写字楼

完：听完 看完 写完 念完 完全

定：决定 一定 定居 定期 定时 预定 一言为定

赛：球赛 预赛 决赛 赛场 赛车 赛马 赛跑
篮球赛 足球赛

军：军人 军校 军区 军医 军服 空军 海军
陆(lù)军

写：写信 写作 写字 写法 大写 小写 书写
手写体

茶：喝茶 茶馆儿 花茶 红茶 龙井茶 奶茶 早茶
茶杯 茶座 茶色

花：花园 花篮 花布 花衣服 开花 花朵 花草
花费 花钱 花时间

草：草地 草坪(píng) 小草

英：英国 英语 英文 英镑 英里

黄：黄色 黄瓜 黄油 金黄色

二、认读下列句子
Read the Following Sentences.

1. 北京的秋天不冷也不热，比较凉快，可是冬天太冷了。

2. 昨天他们坐船在西湖游览了一上午。

3. 我准备在这儿学习一年汉语，一年以后做什么现在还没决定。

4. 在寒冷的冬天，他也一样洗冷水澡，还常常跟朋友一起去冬泳。

5. 新的学生宿舍又干净又便宜，还有全套的家具，我对这儿的条件很满意。

6. 上星期我去看了一场演出，坐在最前边，演员们的表演看得清清楚楚。

7. 春天来了，花园里开满了花，特别漂亮。

8. 在马路上骑车,不要太快,一定要注意交通安全。

9. 全国篮球比赛,上海队得了冠军。

10. 长江和黄河是中国最大的两条河。

11. 他说他一定能想办法把洗衣机修(xiū, to repair)好,我看他是在吹牛。

12. 我爸爸常去那个茶馆儿喝茶。那儿红茶、绿茶、花茶都有,特别是那儿的龙井茶不错。

13. 这些苹果、香蕉、黄瓜,还有茶叶,都是在那个超市买的,花了我一百多块钱。

14. 我觉得汉语跟英语一样,语法比较简单,但是汉字比较难。

15. 记生字、写汉字都要注意学习方法,要注意每个汉字与它(tā)们的意思和读音有什么关系(guānxi relation)。

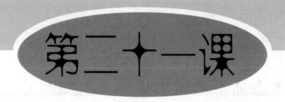

第二十一课

基本知识
Rudiments of Chinese Characters

多音字
The Polyphonic Characters

同一个字形有两个或两个以上的读音,人们称这样的字为多音字。如:"长"在"长短"中读 cháng,在"长大"中读 zhǎng;"觉"在"睡觉"中读 jiào,在"觉得"中读 jué。

Those characters that have more than two pronunciations are known as polyphonic characters. E. g. 长 in 长(cháng)短 and 长(zhǎng)大;觉 in 睡觉(jiào) and 觉(jué)得.

用同一个字形表示几个意义不同的字,这无疑节省了汉字,可以少造一些字,但同时也给学习汉字带来了一定的困难,所以我们在学习汉字时要注意加以区别。

Polysemous characters help reduce the total number of characters, but give rise to the difficulties in distinguishing one character from another. Learners are advised to be aware of the dissimilitude of them.

生字词表
List of New Characters and Words

1.	丝	sī	silk, thread-like thing
	丝绸	sīchóu	silk
2.	级	jí	grade
	年级	niánjí	grade
	初级	chūjí	elementary, primary
	中级	zhōngjí	middle level
	高级	gāojí	senior, high-level
3.	纸	zhǐ	paper
	一张纸	yì zhāng zhǐ	a piece of paper
	餐巾纸	cānjīnzhǐ	paper napkin
4.	红	hóng	red
	红色	hóngsè	red
5.	绿	lǜ	green
	绿色	lǜsè	green
6.	绩	jì	achievement
	成绩	chéngjì	result
7.	练	liàn	to practise
	练习	liànxí	to practise, exercise
8.	系	xì	department
	中文系	Zhōngwén Xì	Chinese department
	关系	guānxi	relation, bearing
	没关系	méi guānxi	It doesn't matter.
	联系	liánxì	to contact, connection
9.	紧	jǐn	tight
	太紧了	tài jǐn le	too tight
10.	远	yuǎn	far
	永远	yǒngyuǎn	always, forever
11.	还	①huán	to return
	还书	huán shū	to return a book
		②hái	still, even more, also
	还是	háishi	still, or, had better

12.	进	jìn	to enter
	请进	qǐng jìn	Come in, please!
	进来	jìnlai	to come in
	进去	jìnqu	to go in
	进入	jìnrù	to enter
	进口	jìnkǒu	to import
13.	过	guò	to cross, to pass, (*verbal suffix*)
	过去	guòqù	the past, to go over
	过去	guòqu	to go past
	不过	búguò	but
14.	送	sòng	to send, to deliver
	送给	sòng gěi	to give, to offer
15.	迎	yíng	to greet, to welcome
	迎接	yíngjiē	to meet, to greet
16.	边	biān	side
	前边	qiánbiān	front
	后边	hòubiān	back
	上边	shàngbiān	above
	下边	xiàbiān	beneath
	里边	lǐbiān	inside
	外边	wàibiān	outside
	东边	dōngbiān	east
	这边	zhèbiān	over here
	一边…	yìbiān…	(two actions) taking place at
	一边…	yìbiān…	the same time
17.	道	dào	way, principle
	道理	dàolǐ	reason, principle, truth
18.	遍	biàn	all over, time
19.	通	tōng	through, open, to go through
	通过	tōngguò	to pass through, by means of
	通知	tōngzhī	to inform, to notify
20.	遇	yù	to meet (by chance), to encounter
	遇见	yùjiàn	to meet
21.	建	jiàn	to establish
	建立	jiànlì	to establish
	建设	jiànshè	to build, to construct

22. 延	yán	to prolong
延长	yáncháng	to prolong
23. 病	bìng	sick
病人	bìngrén	patient
生病	shēng bìng	to fall sick
看病	kàn bìng	to see a doctor
病假	bìngjià	sick leave
24. 瘦	shòu	thin, tight
瘦肉	shòuròu	lean meat
25. 疼	téng	to have aches and pains
头疼	tóu téng	headache, feel disgusted
26. 痛	tòng	pain
痛快	tòngkuài	thoroughly enjoyable
27. 院	yuàn	yard
医院	yīyuàn	hospital
学院	xuéyuàn	college, institute
28. 随	suí	to follow
随便	suíbiàn	as you like
随身听	suíshēntīng	walkman
29. 附	fù	to attach
附近	fùjìn	nearby
30. 阿	ā	ah
阿拉伯	Ālābó	Arab
31. 都	①dōu	all, already, even
都来了	dōu lái le	Everybody is here.
	②dū	capital
首都	shǒudū	capital
32. 邮	yóu	post
邮票	yóupiào	stamp
电子邮件	diànzǐ yóujiàn	e-mail
电子邮箱	diànzǐ yóuxiāng	mailbox
33. 部	bù	department, part
全部	quánbù	all, whole
部分	bùfen	part, section
34. 犬	quǎn	dog

35.	狗	gǒu	dog
	小狗	xiǎo gǒu	puppy
36.	猫	māo	cat
37.	猪	zhū	pig
	猪肉	zhūròu	pork
38.	猜	cāi	to guess
	猜想	cāixiǎng	to guess, to suppose
39.	哭	kū	to cry
	大哭	dà kū	to cry bitterly

生字的结构和书写
The Structures and Writing of the New Characters

 绞丝旁　jiǎo sī páng　The Radical of 纟

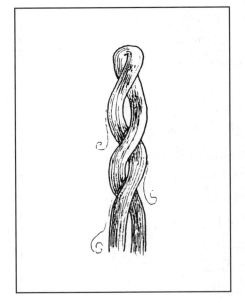

古字像一束丝的样子。"纟"做形旁的字一般与丝（包括棉、麻、毛及化学纤维）一类事物有关,有的表示颜色。偏旁"纟"在字的左侧。在字的下部写做"糸",称为"丝字底"。

The ancient written form of the radical is in the shape of tied silk. When used as a radical it is generally related to silk, thread of cotton, flax or wool, chemical fibre, and even colour. It often stands on the left of a character, but sometimes it may be written as 糸 used at the lower part of a character, hence known as "a bottom silk sign".

1 丝　　sī　silk, thread-like thing

丝绸　sīchóu　silk

①纟　②纟　③一

2 级　　jí　grade

年级　niánjí　grade
初级　chūjí　elementary, primary
中级　zhōngjí　middle level
高级　gāojí　senior, high-level

①纟　②及(jí) | ノ | 乃 | 及 |

3 纸　　zhǐ　paper

一张纸　yì zhāng zhǐ　a piece of paper
餐巾纸　cānjīnzhǐ　paper napkin

①纟　②氏(shì) | ⌐ | ⎩ | 𠂆 | 氏 |

4 红　　hóng　red

红色　hóngsè　red

①纟　②工

5 绿　　lǜ　green

绿色　lǜsè　green

①纟　②录(lǜ) | ⁊ | ⁊ | ⁊ | 录 | 录 | 录 | 录 |

6 绩　　jì　achievement

成绩　chéngjì　result

①纟　②+③责(zé) | 一 | 二 | 圭 | 主 | 责 |

7 练　liàn　to practise

练习　liànxí　to practise, exercise

1	2

①纟　②东

糸　丝字底　sī zì dǐ　The Radical of 糸

8 系　xì　department

1	
2	

中文系　Zhōngwén Xì　Chinese department

关系　guānxi　relation, bearing

没关系　méi guānxi　It doesn't matter.

联系　liánxì　to contact, connection

①一　②糸

9 紧　jǐn　tight

太紧了　tài jǐn le　too tight

1	2
3	

① "　| ' | " |　②又　③糸

辶　走之旁　zǒu zhī páng　The Radical of 辶

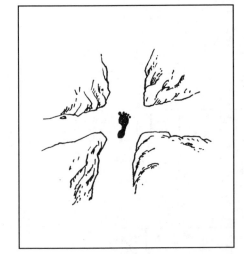

古字像一个十字路口中间有一只向前走去的脚（止）。路上有脚，表示行走，所以"辶"做形旁的字一般和行走的意思有关。走之旁在字的左下侧。

The ancient written form of the radical is in the shape of a forward foot at the crossroads. Therefore it carries the sense of "walking". It is used at the lower left of a character.

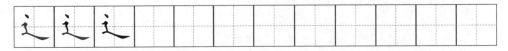

⑩ 远   yuǎn   far

永远   yǒngyuǎn   always, forever
①元   ②辶

⑪ 还   ①huán   to return

还书   huán shū   to return a book
②hái   still, even more, also
还是   háishi   still, or, had better
①不   ②辶

⑫ 进   jìn   to enter

请进   qǐng jìn   Come in, please!
进来   jìnlai   to come in
进去   jìnqu   to go in
进入   jìnrù   to enter
进口   jìnkǒu   to import
①井   ②辶

⑬ 过   guò   to cross, to pass, (*verbal suffix*)

过去   guòqù   the past, to go over
过去   guòqu   to go past
不过   búguò   but
①寸   ②辶

⑭ 送   sòng   to send, to deliver

送给   sòng gěi   to give, to offer
①关   ②辶

⑮ 迎   yíng   to greet, to welcome

迎接   yíngjiē   to meet, to greet
①卬   ㇒ 卬 卬 卬   ②辶

16 边

biān　side

前边　qiánbiān　front
后边　hòubiān　back
上边　shàngbiān　above
下边　xiàbiān　beneath
里边　lǐbiān　inside
外边　wàibiān　outside
东边　dōngbiān　east
这边　zhèbiān　over here
一边……一边……
yìbiān…yìbiān…(two actions)taking palce at the same time
①力　②辶

17 道

dào　way,principle

道理　dàolǐ　reason,principle,truth
①首　②辶

18 遍

biàn　all over,time

①扁(biǎn)| 尸 | 户 | 肩 | 肩 | 扁 | 扁 |　②辶

19 通

tōng　through,open,to go through

通过　tōngguò　to pass through,by means of
通知　tōngzhī　to inform,to notify
①甬(yǒng)| 丆 | 丒 | 甬 |　　②辶

20 遇

yù　to meet (by chance),to encounter

遇见　yùjiàn　to meet
①禺(yú)| 日 | 旦 | 咼 | 禺 | 禺 | 禺 |　②辶

廴　建字底　jiàn zì dǐ　The Radical of 廴

"廴"的下面一直向右拐延长，表示长行的意思，"廴"做偏旁的字很少。

Its final stroke extends to the lower right of a character. There is only a small number of characters containing such a radical.

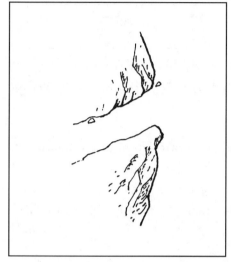

廴 廴

21 建　jiàn　to establish

建立　jiànlì　to establish

建设　jiànshè　to build, to construct

① 聿 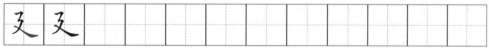　② 廴

22 延　yán　to prolong

延长　yáncháng　to prolong

① 正 　② 廴

疒　　病字头　　bìng zì tóu　　The Radical of 疒

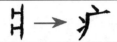

古字像大汗淋漓的人躺在床上的样子,意思是"生病","疒"做形旁的字一般和疾病有关。

> The ancient written form of the radical is in the shape of a man dripping with sweat in bed, suggesting "a sick person". When used as a radical it is often related to "illness".

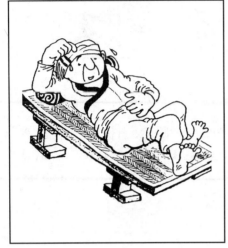

疒	疒	疒	疒	疒							

㉓ 病　　bìng　　sick

病人　bìngrén　　patient
生病　shēng bìng　to fall sick
看病　kàn bìng　to see a doctor
病假　bìngjià　sick leave

①疒　②丙(bǐng)

一	厂	厅	丙	丙

㉔ 瘦　　shòu　　thin, tight

瘦肉　shòuròu　lean meat

①疒　②+③叟(sǒu)

ノ	⺁	⺈	⺈	⺈	臼	申	叟

㉕ 疼　　téng　　to have aches and pains

头疼　tóu téng　headache, to feel disgusted

①疒　②冬

26 痛　tòng　pain

痛快　tòngkuai　thoroughly enjoyable

①疒　②甬

阝　左耳旁　zuǒ ěr páng　The Radical of 阝

左耳旁"阝"是"阜"做偏旁的简化。古汉字"阜"像山坡的样子，上端的一横是平顶，下部是延绵起伏的丘陵。本义是土山，所以"阝"在左侧做形旁的字一般与山坡或高地有关。

The left radical 阝 is the simplified 阜 as a side component. Its ancient written form is in the shape of cliffs with a flat top and undulating hills at the lower part. When functioning as a radical on the left of a character, it is related to mountain slope or upland.

阝	阝											

27 院　yuàn　yard

医院　yīyuàn　hospital

学院　xuéyuàn　college, institute

①阝　②完

28 随　suí　to follow

随便　suíbiàn　as you like

随身听　suíshēntīng　walkman

①阝　②有　③辶

29 附　　fù　to attach

附近　fùjìn　nearby

①阝　②＋③付（fù）| 亻 | 付 |

30 阿　　ā　ah

阿拉伯　Ālābó　Arab

①阝　②可

阝　　右耳边　yòu ěr biān　The Radical of 阝

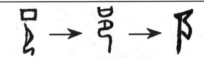

右耳旁"阝"是"邑"做偏旁的简化,古汉字"邑"在表示区域的"口"下加跪坐的人形来表示人的所居之处。"阝"在右侧做形旁的字一般与城邑或地方有关。

The right radical 阝 is the simplified 邑 as a side component. Its ancient written form is in the shape of 口 with a man on his knees. Thus it is related to "town" or "place".

31 都　①dōu　all, already, even

都来了　dōu lái le　Every boby is hare.

②dū　capital

首都　shǒudū　capital

①者（zhě）| 一 | 十 | 土 | 耂 | 耂 | 者 | 者 | 者 |　②阝

32 邮　　yóu　post

邮票　yóupiào　stamp

电子邮件　*diànzǐ yóujiàn*　e-mail

电子邮箱　*diànzǐ yóuxiāng*　mailbox

| 1 | 2 |

①由（yóu）丨　冂　冂　由　由　　②阝

33 部　*bù*　department, part

| 1 | 3 |
| 2 | |

全部　*quánbù*　all, whole

部分　*bùfen*　part, section

①立　　②口　　③阝

犭　反犬旁　*fǎn quǎn páng*　The Radical of 犭

"犭"是"犬"的变体。"犬"做形旁的汉字一般与狗和兽类有关。"犬"在字的左边时写做"犭"，称为"反犬旁"，在字的下面写做"犬"。

犭 derived from the pictographic 犬 as a radical is often related to "dog" or "animal". When standing on the left of a character, it is written as 犭 known as "the reversed dog sign". It can also be used at the lower part of a character in the form of 犬.

| 犭 | 犭 | 犭 | | | | | | | | | |

34 犬　*quǎn*　dog

| 大 | 犬 |

| 1 |

35 狗　*gǒu*　dog

小狗　*xiǎo gǒu*　puppy

| 1 | 2 |
| | 3 |

①犭　　②+③句（jù）丿　勹　句

36 猫　　māo　cat

①犭　　②＋③苗(miáo) 艹 苗

1 | 2
3

37 猪　　zhū　pig

猪肉　zhūròu　pork
①犭　　②者

1 | 2

38 猜　　cāi　to guess

猜想　cāixiǎng　to guess，to suppose
①犭　　②青

1 | 2

39 哭　　kū　to cry

大哭　dà kū　to cry bitterly
①口　　②口　　③犬

1 | 2
3

认读词、词组和句子
Read the Following Words，Phrases and Sentences

一、认读词、词组
Read the Following Words and Phrases.

丝：真丝　丝袜　铁丝　肉丝

级：年级　高级　中级　班级　等级　上级　下级

纸：报纸　纸片　纸巾　一张纸　纸币　信纸

红：红色　红茶　红旗　红笔　红灯　红绿灯　红花
　　脸红　口红　红烧鱼

绿：绿色　绿茶　绿灯　绿化

系:中文系　外语系　英语系　历史系　法律系
　　计算机系

远:远方　远山　长远　远近　跳远　远郊

还:还书　还给　还钱

进:进来　进去　进城　进口　进步　进度

过:过去　过来　过年　过日子　不过　过期　过时
　　通过　路过　难过

送:送给　送来　送礼　送货　接送　欢送　送别　送行

边:上边　下边　里边　外边　东边　西边　南边
　　北边　前边　后边　两边　身边　河边　海边

道:知道　道路　道理　铁道　人行道

通:通车　通航　通信　通知　通过　通风　通电话
　　地下通道

遇:遇见　遇到　相遇

建:建立　建成　建交　建军

病:病人　生病　胃病　病房　病床　病假　看病
　　心脏病　病情

瘦:瘦小　瘦长　肥瘦　胖瘦　瘦高个

疼:头疼　脚疼　胃疼　牙疼　肚(dù)子疼　心疼

院:医院　住院　出院　电影院　四合院　学院　院长

随:随身　随手　随口　随时　随地

邮:邮票　邮局　邮包　邮件　邮费　集邮

二、认读下列句子
Read the Following Sentences.

1. 这种丝绸衣服穿着很凉快。

2. 他现在是中文系一年级学生,成绩不错,进入中级班
　　学习应该没问题。

3. 每个人的爱好不一样,有人喜欢喝红茶。南方人一般喜欢喝绿茶,北方人比较喜欢喝花茶。

4. 我今天去医院看病的时候遇到了王老师,他在那儿住院,他比以前瘦多了。

5. 那个病人疼得快哭了。

6. 这个学院是一年前刚建立的。

7. 附近有没有邮局?我想买几张邮票。

8. 我借的那些书已经全部还给图书馆了。

9. 上次考试时他太紧张了,所以考得不好,没有通过。

10. 北京是中国的首都,欢迎你们来北京旅游。

11. 时间太紧了,还有很多题没做完呢,再延长半个小时吧。

12. 昨天晚上我跟朋友一起去酒吧,一边喝酒,一边聊天,聊得很痛快。

13. 大部分学生我已经通知过了,还有两个阿拉伯学生没找到,他们不在房间。

14. 这只小狗是我一个朋友上个星期送给我的,不过来到我家以后就生病了,不爱吃东西。

15. 绿化北京,建设北京,迎接 2008 年奥(ào)运会!

16. A:昨天是小王女朋友的生日,可是他忘了。有一句话,他女朋友哭着对他说了三遍,你猜,她说的是什么?

    B:是什么?我猜不着。

    A:"我永远也不想再见到你!"

17. 这些水果都是进口的。

18. 小姐,请给我们拿几张餐巾纸来。

19. A:请进,让你久(jiǔ, a long time)等了。

    B:没关系。

20. 我们俩通过 e-mail 常常联系,关系一直很好。

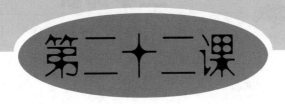

基本知识

Rudiments of Chinese Characters

同音字

Homonyms

在学习汉字的过程中，我们会发现，有些汉字的字音相同，字义却不同，如：首—手、作—座、练—炼等，人们把这样的字叫做同音字。现代汉语一共只有 435 个独立音节，如果加上声调，也只有 1,152 个音节，而汉字有几万个（常用的有三千多个），要用这么少的音节写出这么多汉字，就会有很多同音字。如：读"shì"这个音，我们学过的就有：士、示、世、市、试、视、是、室等，所以我们在学习汉字时，要培养区别同音字的习惯。

One character can be the same in pronunciation but different in meaning from another, e.g. 首 and 手，作 and 座，练 and 炼. They are known as homonyms. There are 435 independent syllables, or 1,152 syllables in varied tones in modern Chinese. However the number of characters totals up to several ten thousand (including more than three thousand commonly-used characters), therefore the number of Chinese homonyms is unavoidably great. For example, of the characters that share the pronunciation "shì" in the previous lessons there are 士，示，世，市，试，视，是 and 室 etc. Therefore it would be good for us to differentiate one homonym from another.

生字词表
List of New Characters and Words

1.	园	yuán	garden
	公园	gōngyuán	park
	果园	guǒyuán	orchard
2.	图	tú	picture
	图书馆	túshūguǎn	library
	地图	dìtú	map
3.	因	yīn	because, cause
	因为	yīnwèi	because
4.	圆	yuán	round, circle
	圆珠笔	yuánzhūbǐ	ball-pen
5.	围	wéi	to surround
	围巾	wéijīn	scarf
6.	医	yī	to cure
	医生	yīshēng	doctor
	医学	yīxué	medical studies
	中医	zhōngyī	traditional Chinese medicine
7.	匹	pǐ	(a measure word)
	一匹马	yì pǐ mǎ	a horse
8.	影	yǐng	shadow, picture, movie
	电影	diànyǐng	film
	电影院	diànyǐngyuàn	cinema
9.	彩	cǎi	colour
	彩色	cǎisè	colourful
10.	须	xū	should
	必须	bìxū	should, must
11.	参	cān	to participate, to consult
	参加	cānjiā	to attend, to participate

12. 往	wǎng	toward
往东走	wǎng dōng zǒu	to go eastward
13. 街	jiē	street
街道	jiēdào	street
街区	jiēqū	block
步行街	bùxíngjiē	pedestrian street
14. 得	①de	[used after a verb or an adjective to introduce a complement of result, possibility or degree]
写得很好	xiě de hěn hǎo	to have written well
	②dé	to get
得到	dédào	to obtain
	③děi	need, must
你得去	nǐ děi qù	You should go.
15. 考	kǎo	to examine
考试	kǎoshì	examination
考虑	kǎolù	to think over, to consider
16. 者	zhě	(suffix, the one who...)
记者	jìzhě	journalist
作者	zuòzhě	author
读者	dúzhě	reader
17. 商	shāng	commerce, to discuss
商业	shāngyè	business
电子商务	diànzǐ shāngwù	electronic commerce
商量	shāngliang	to discuss
18. 离	lí	to leave, from
离开	líkāi	to leave
19. 旁	páng	side
旁边	pángbiān	by the side of
20. 就	jiù	just
21. 同	tóng	together
同学	tóngxué	fellow student
同屋	tóngwū	roommate
同时	tóngshí	at the same time, meanwhile

相同	xiāngtóng	identical, alike
不同	bùtóng	different from
22. 周	zhōu	circuit, all around, week
周围	zhōuwéi	surroundings, all around
23. 网	wǎng	net
网球	wǎngqiú	tennis
网络	wǎngluò	network
网吧	wǎngbā	Internet café, cyberbar
网站	wǎngzhàn	website
上网	shàng wǎng	on line
24. 各	gè	each
各种各样	gè zhǒng gè yàng	all kinds
25. 务	wù	affairs
医务所	yīwùsuǒ	clinic
服务	fúwù	service, to serve
服务员	fúwùyuán	attendant, waiter
26. 备	bèi	to prepare
准备	zhǔnbèi	to prepare
27. 处	chù	place, office
到处	dàochù	everywhere
好处	hǎochù	benefit, advantage
坏处	huàichù	harm, disadvantage
28. 夏	xià	summer
夏天	xiàtiān	summer
29. 教	①jiāo	to teach, to instruct
教书	jiāo shū	to teach
	②jiào	to teach, religion
教室	jiàoshì	classroom
教育	jiàoyù	to educate, education
教授	jiàoshòu	professor
30. 收	shōu	to receive
收拾	shōushi	to tidy up
收音机	shōuyīnjī	radio

31.	散	①sǎn	to disperse
	散步	②sànbù	to take a walk
32.	敢	gǎn	dare
33.	数	①shù	number
	数学	shùxué	mathematics
	数量	shùliàng	quantity
	多数	duōshù	majority, most
	少数	shǎoshù	a small number
		②shǔ	to count
	数一数	shǔ yi shǔ	to count
34.	包	bāo	to wrap
	面包	miànbāo	bread
	书包	shūbāo	satchel, schoolbag
35.	句	jù	sentence
	句子	jùzi	sentence
36.	左	zuǒ	left
	左边	zuǒbiān	left
37.	右	yòu	right
	右边	yòubiān	right
	左右	zuǒyòu	about, more or less

生字的结构和书写

The Structures and Writing of the New Characters

口　　方框　　fāng kuàng　　The Radical of 口

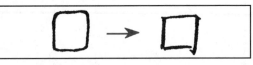

"口"是"国"的古体字。古字像一个四面围起来的方形的围墙。"口"做形旁的字一般与界限和范围、裹束一类事物有关。

口 (a squared wall), an ancient written form of 国, is related to "boundary" or "encircle".

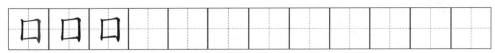

口 口 口

① 园　yuán　garden

公园　gōngyuán　park
果园　guǒyuán　orchard

①+②+③　丨 冂 园 园

② 图　tú　picture

图书馆　túshūguǎn　library
地图　dìtú　map

①+②+③　丨 冂 图 图

3 因　yīn　because, cause

因为　yīnwèi　because

①＋②＋③　门　冈　因

4 圆　yuán　round, circle

圆珠笔　yuánzhūbǐ　ball-pen

①＋②＋③　门　圆　圆

5 围　wéi　to surround

围巾　wéijīn　scarf

①＋②＋③　门　冂　冃　冐　围　围

匚　区字框　qū zì kuàng　The Radical of 匚

古字像一个方形的箱子。箱底在左，箱口向右。箱子是用于收藏东西的器具，所以"匚"做形旁的字一般与盛物的器具或收藏一类事物有关。

The ancient written form of 匚 is in the shape of a box with its bottom on the left and its opening on the right. As a radical of a character it is related to "container" or "collection".

匚　匚

6 医　yī　to cure

医生　yīshēng　doctor

医学　yīxué　medical studies

中医　zhōngyī　traditional Chinese medicine

①一　②矢　③乚

7 匹　pǐ　（a measure word）

一匹马　yì pǐ mǎ　a horse

①一　②儿　③乚

彡　三撇　sān piě　The Radical of　彡

"彡"是一个象形符号，一般在字的右侧，有时也可在左侧。"彡"做形旁的字常和毛须、光芒等有关。

彡 as a pictographic radical is often related to "hair" or "rays". It can be used on the right or the left of a character.

8 影　yǐng　shadow, picture, movie

电影　diànyǐng　film

电影院　diànyǐngyuàn　cinema

①+②景（jǐng）日 | 景　③彡

9 彩　cǎi　colour

彩色　cǎisè　colourful

①+②采（cǎi）丿 | ⺥ | 采　③彡

10 须　xū　should

必须　bìxū　should, must

| 1 | 2 |

①彡　②页

11 参　cān　to participate, to consult

参加　cānjiā　to attend, to participate

| 1 |
| 2 |
| 3 |

①厶　②大　③彡

彳　双人旁　shuāng rén páng　The Radical of 彳

"彳"是象形字"行"的左半边。"行"像十字路口的形状,象形字"行"见上册第98页,所以"彳"做形旁的字一般与道路或行走有关。双人旁总在字的左侧。

彳 is the half of the pictographic 行. When functioning as a left radical of a character (see page 98, Textboook I) it is generally related to "road" or "walk".

12 往　wǎng　toward

往东走　wǎng dōng zǒu　to go eastward

| 1 | 2 |

①彳　②主

13 街　jiē　street

街道　jiēdào　street

街区　jiēqū　block
步行街　bùxíngjiē　pedestrian street

1	2	3

①彳　②圭　③亍

14 得

①de　［used after a verb or an adjective to introduce a complement of result, possibility or degree］

写得很好　xiě de hěn hǎo　to have wirtten well

②dé　to get

得到　dédào　to obtain

③děi　need, must

你得去　nǐ děi qù　You should go.

①彳　②日　③一　④寸

耂　老字头　lǎo zì tóu　The Radical of 耂

象形字"老"见上册第114页。包含"老字头"的字常与老人有关。

The pictographic script 老（see page114, Book I）as a radical is often related to "an aged person".

耂	耂	耂	耂								

15 考

kǎo　to examine

1	
	2

考试　kǎoshì　examination
考虑　kǎolù　to think over, to consider

①耂　②丂　| 一 | 丂 |

16 者

zhě　（*suffix*, the one who...）

记者　jìzhě　journalist

作者　zuòzhě　author
读者　dúzhě　reader
①耂　②日

二　高字头　gāo zì tóu　The Radical of 亠

人 → 亠

意义不明，取字形表部首。我们学过的汉字有"京、高"等。

It acts as a head sign of a group of radicals and is obscure in meaning.

亠　亠

17 商　shāng　commerce，to discuss

商业　shāngyè　business
电子商务　diànzǐ shāngwù　electronic commerce
商量　shāngliang　to discuss

①亠　②丷　③冋　| 丨 | 冂 | 冂 | 冋 |

18 离　lí　to leave，from

离开　líkāi　to leave

①亠　②凶　③禸　| 冂 | 内 | 禸 |

19 旁　páng　side

旁边　pángbiān　by the side of

①亠　②丷　③冖　④方

20 就　jiù　just

①十②京　③尤（yóu）　| 一 | ナ | 尢 | 尤 |

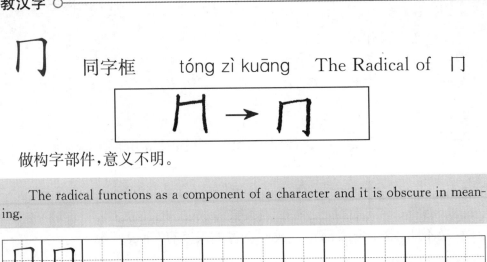

冂　同字框　tóng zì kuāng　The Radical of 冂

做构字部件，意义不明。

The radical functions as a component of a character and it is obscure in meaning.

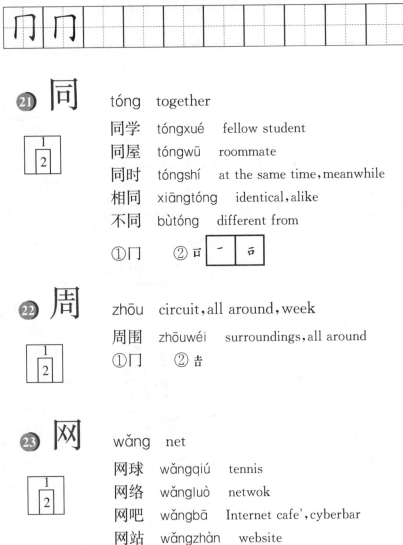

21 同　tóng　together

同学　tóngxué　fellow student
同屋　tóngwū　roommate
同时　tóngshí　at the same time, meanwhile
相同　xiāngtóng　identical, alike
不同　bùtóng　different from

①冂　②口 ［一］［口］

22 周　zhōu　circuit, all around, week

周围　zhōuwéi　surroundings, all around

①冂　②吉

23 网　wǎng　net

网球　wǎngqiú　tennis
网络　wǎngluò　netwok
网吧　wǎngbā　Internet cafe', cyberbar
网站　wǎngzhàn　website
上网　shàng wǎng　on line

①冂　②㐅 ［丿］［㐅］［㐅］［㐅］

夂　折文旁　zhé wén páng　The Radical of 夂

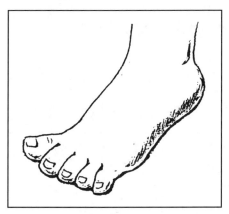

古字像脚,但现在带折文旁的字与脚已无关系,只是做构字部件。

The ancient written form of the radical is in the shape of human foot, but functioning as a radical now it does not suggest anything of that.

夂	夂	夂									

24 各 gè　each

各种各样　gè zhǒng gè yàng　all kinds
①夂　②口

25 务 wù　affairs

医务所　yīwùsuǒ　clinic
服务　fúwù　service, to serve
服务员　fúwùyuán　attendant, waiter
①夂　②力

26 备 bèi　to prepare

准备　zhǔnbèi　to prepare
①夂　②田

27 处 chù　place

到处　dàochù　everywhere
好处　hǎochù　benefit, advantage
坏处　huàichù　harm, disadvantage
①夂　②卜　(注意"处"与"外"的区别)

28 夏　xià　summer

1	
2	
3	

夏天　xiàtiān　summer

①一　②自　③夂　（注意"夏"与"复"的区别）

夂　反文边　fǎn wén biān　The Radical of　夂

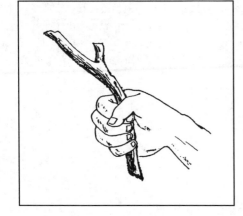

夂 → 𠬝 → 夂

古字像手拿棍棒责打的样子。"夂"做形旁的字，常跟人的动作或行为有关。反文边一般在字的右侧。

The ancient written form of the radical depicts someone punishing someone else with a club. It is related to "action" or "behaviour" when used on the right of a character.

夂	夂	夂	夂									

29 教

1	2

①jiāo　to teach, to instruct

教书　jiāo shū　to teach

②jiào　to teach, religion

教室　jiàoshì　classroom

教育　jiàoyù　to educate, education

教授　jiàoshòu　professor

①孝(xiào)

⺹	⺹	孝	孝

②夂

30 收

1	2

shōu　to receive

收拾　shōushi　to tidy up

收音机　shōuyīnjī　radio

①丩　②夂

31 散　sàn　to disperse

散步　sànbù　to take a walk

| 1 | 3 |
| 2 | |

①⼟　②月　③⼂

32 敢　gǎn　dare

| 1 | 2 |

①耳　[⼀ | 耳]　②⼂

33 数

①shù　number

数学　shùxué　mathematics
数量　shùliàng　quantity
多数　duōshù　majority, most
少数　shǎoshù　a small number

②shǔ　to count

数一数　shǔ yi shǔ　to count

| 1 | 3 |
| 2 | |

①+②娄 [米 | 娄]　③⼂

勹　包字框　bāo zì kuāng　The Radical of 勹

古字像人体和手臂弯曲抱住东西。"勹"做形旁的字常与弯曲身子等意义有关。

The ancient written form of the radical is in the shape of a bending human body or curved hands to hold something. It is related to "bend over".

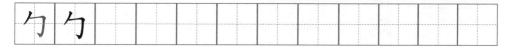

34 包   bāo   to wrap

面包   miànbāo   bread

书包   shūbāo   satchel, schoolbag

①勹   ②巳(sì) | ㄱ | ㄱ | 巳 | (注意与"己"和"已"的区别)

35 句   jù   sentence

句子   jùzi   sentence

①勹   ②口

ナ   有字旁   yǒu zì páng   The Radical of ナ

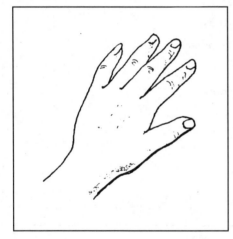

古字像左手三个指头的形状,本义是左手的意思。"ナ"做形旁的字常与手有关。

The ancient character in the shape of three fingers of a left hand. Originally it meant "a left hand", now is related to "hands" when used as a radical.

36 左   zuǒ   left

左边   zuǒbiān   left

①ナ   ②工

37 右   yòu   right

右边   yòubiān   right

左右   zuǒyòu   about, more or less

①ナ   ②口

认读词、词组和句子
Read the Following Words，Phrases and Sentences

一、认读词、词组
Read the Following Words and Phrases.

园:公园　花园　校园　果园　动物园　圆明园

图:图书　一张地图　中国地图　世界地图　图画
图书馆

因:因为　因此　原因

医:中医　西医　医学　牙医　医院　医师　医书
名医

影:电影院　影片　合影　人影

参:参加　参观　参军

考:期中考试　期末考试　考场　考古　考生　考上
思考　考虑

者:记者　作者　读者　或者　学者

商:商业　商店　商人　商场　商品　商量

离:离别　离家　离校　离职　分离　脱离

旁:旁边　两旁　路旁　声旁　身旁

同:同志　同屋　同学　同桌　同样　不同　同意
同行　同事　共同

周:周末　四周　周年　周岁

网:通信网　交通网　网民　网友　网址　网虫　网校
网上聊天　网上购物　因特网

各:各人　各地　各国　各种　各个　各处　各级

务:服务　公务员　家务　商务　职务　业务

处：各处　四处　用处　好处　坏处　住处　售票处
办事处　停车处

夏：夏天　夏季　夏日

教：教室　教师　教学　教练　请教　家教　外教
教堂　天主教　教会　信教

收：收到　收入　收集

散：散会　散场　散开　分散

数：(shù) 数词　数字　人数　次数　单数　复数　岁数
数码相机

包：面包　书包　钱包　邮包

左：左手　左右　往左拐　左脚　左思右想

二、认读下列句子
Read the Following Sentences.

1. 昨天,有人来教室找你,他说他是记者,大概三十岁
左右。

2. 因为教室离宿舍楼很近,所以我每天走着去上课。

3. 夏天的时候,很多人在这条街道两旁散步。

4. 上次的语法考试我考得不太好,只得了七十分,我数
了数,好几个句子的语法都写错了。

5. 最近电影院的电影都不是彩色的,都是黑白的老电
影,我准备去买两张票。

6. 左边那个面包房里有各种各样的面包,你去那儿
买吧。

7. 去年夏天我参加了那个网校的学习。

8. 上星期我们参观了那个城市,那儿的街道真干净。

9. 那个公园旁边有一个很大的商店,周围还有几个小
商店。

10. 夏子上次语法考试得了九十分。

11. 我昨天在网上收到了我哥哥发来的 e-mail, 我准备今天晚上上网吧给他回封信。

12. 我得到了我同屋的很多帮助, 在他生日的时候, 我一定得买件礼物谢谢他。

13. 周末去首都图书馆的读者很多, 所以我必须早点儿去, 去晚了就没座位了。

14. 王教授的教学方法跟其他老师的完全不同。

15. 那时候, 我想来中国学习中医, 可是我不敢告诉我爸爸, 我知道他不会同意, 所以只好跟我妈妈商量。

16. 现在网吧到处都是, 网民数量也一天比一天多。网络带给人们的好处很多, 但也不是完全没有坏处。

17. 我正在考虑, 要不要再去买条长围巾。

第二十三课

基本知识
Rudiments of Chinese Characters

汉字的造字方法(三)
The Formation of Chinese Characters (C)

会意字
Associative Characters

用两个或两个以上的部件所表示的意义合在一起表示该字意义的合体字叫会意字。会意字两个或两个以上的部件都是形旁。通过观察会意字的形旁,我们常常可以猜出该字的大概意思。例如:

> Associative Chinese characters are those written symbols of which the meaning is based on the lexical significance of the two or more components that they are formed by. The two or more components of such a character can all function as a pictographic radical. For example:

休(xiū):人在树下,表示休息的意思。

休 symbolizes a person under a tree, hence it means "take a rest".

众(zhòng):三个人表示人很多,如"观众、听众"等。

众 symbolizes three people, hence it means "a great number of people".

嵩(sōng):用"山"和"高"表示山高。

嵩 symbolizes high mountains jointly expressed by "a mountain" and "high".

鸣(míng)：用"鸟"和"口"，表示鸣叫。

鸣 means "birds' singing" jointly expressed by "a bird" and "mouth".

尘(chén)：用"小"和"土"表示灰尘。

尘 means "dust" jointly expressed by "tiny" and "earth".

生字词表

List of New Characters and words

1. 如	rú	if, as if, like, as
如果	rúguǒ	if
比如	bǐrú	for instance
不如	bù rú	not so good as
2. 始	shǐ	to begin
开始	kāishǐ	to begin
3. 妇	fù	woman
妇女	fùnǚ	woman
夫妇	fūfù	husband and wife
4. 从	cóng	from
从……到……	cóng…dào…	from . . . to . . .
从……起	cóng…qǐ	from . . . on
从不	cóngbù	never
从来	cónglái	ever, always
从此	cóngcǐ	from now on, since then
5. 双	shuāng	two, pair
双手	shuāngshǒu	both hands
一双筷子	yì shuāng kuàizi	a pair of chopsticks

6.	林	lín	woods
	树林	shùlín	woods
7.	析	xī	analysis
	分析	fēnxī	analysis
8.	取	qǔ	to get
	取得	qǔdé	to get
9.	烦	fán	annoying
	麻烦	máfan	trouble
10.	改	gǎi	to change
	改变	gǎibiàn	to change
	改正	gǎizhèng	to correct
11.	初	chū	beginning
	初级	chūjí	primary
	初中	chūzhōng	junior middle school
12.	解	jiě	to understand，to undo
	了解	liǎojiě	to understand
	解决	jiějué	to solve，solution
13.	鲜	xiān	fresh，delicious
	新鲜	xīnxiān	fresh
	鲜花	xiānhuā	fresh flowers
14.	位	wèi	seat
	座位	zuòwèi	seat
	位置	wèizhì	seat，place，position
15.	信	xìn	letter，to believe in
	信封	xìnfēng	envelope
	短信	duǎnxìn	note
	相信	xiāngxìn	to believe
	信心	xìnxīn	confidence，faith
16.	冰	bīng	ice
	冰箱	bīngxiāng	refrigerator

	滑冰	huábīng	skating
17.	泪	lèi	tear
	眼泪	yǎnlèi	tear
18.	汽	qì	steam
	汽车	qìchē	automobile
	公共汽车	gōnggòng qìchē	bus
19.	沙	shā	sand
	沙发	shāfā	sofa
	沙漠	shāmò	desert
20.	酒	jiǔ	alcoholic drink
	酒吧	jiǔbā	bar
	葡萄酒	pútaojiǔ	wine
21.	阳	yáng	sun
	太阳	tàiyáng	sun
	阳台	yángtái	balcony
22.	阴	yīn	cloudy
	阴天	yīntiān	cloudy
23.	鸣	míng	to cry
	鸣叫	míngjiào	to cry
24.	利	lì	benefit, sharp
	顺利	shùnlì	smooth
	利用	lìyòng	to use, to make use of
	有利	yǒulì	beneficial, favourable
	流利	liúlì	fluent, smooth
25.	删	shān	to delete
	删去	shānqu	to delete
26.	班	bān	shift
	上班	shàng bān	to go to work
	下班	xià bān	to come off work
	班长	bānzhǎng	monitor
27.	粥	zhōu	porridge
	小米粥	xiǎomǐ zhōu	millet gruel
28.	掰	bāi	to break off
	掰开	bāikāi	to break off

生字的字源和书写
The Origin and Writing of the New Characters

1 如   rú   if, as if, like, as

如果   rúguǒ   if
比如   bǐrú   for instanee
不如   bù rú   not so good as

女＋口 → 如

"口"是主人的命令,女人必须听从使唤。引申为照样、服从的意思。

> Oral instruction from a master makes a woman to obey. Extensively the character means "as usual" or "submit".

如	如								

2 始   shǐ   to begin

开始   kāishǐ   to begin

女＋台 → 始

"台"指"胎儿",人的生命从母胎里开始。引申为开头、开始的意思。

> 台 symbolizes "a human foetus" that develops in the womb. By extension the character means "begin".

始	始	始							

③ 妇 fù woman

妇女 fùnǚ woman
夫妇 fūfù husband and wife

$$女 + 彐 → 妇$$

"彐"是"帚"的简写。一个女人手拿扫帚在打扫,这是家庭主妇的日常工作。

彐 is the simplified form of 帚. A woman with a broom in hand implies that "a housewife does her everyday chore".

妇	妇	妇	妇									

④ 从 cóng from

从……到…… cóng…dào… from … to …
从……起 cóng…qǐ from … on
从不 cóngbù never
从来 cónglái ever, always
从此 cóngcǐ from no won, since then

$$人 + 人 → 从$$

两人一前一后,一人跟着另一人,表示跟从。

从 depicts one person closely followed by the other, in the sense of "follow".

从	从	从	从									

⑤ 双 shuāng two，pair

双手　shuāngshǒu　both hands

一双筷子　yì shuāng kuàizi　a pair of chopsticks

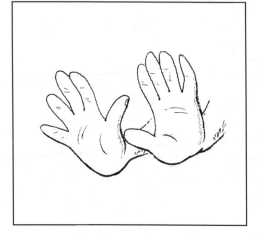

又＋又 → 双

"又"在古文字中表示一只手，两只手在一起就是一双手。本义是两个、一对，现泛指成双的东西。

The ancient written form of 又 is in the shape of a human hand，logically 双 means "two hands". The original meaning of 双 was "a pair"，now it is used in the sense of "both" or "twin".

双	双										

⑥ 林 lín woods

树林　shùlín　woods

木＋木 → 林

两棵树并排在一起，表示树木多，树木多的地方就是树林了。

Two trees that stand side by side imply "many trees" or "woods".

林	林										

7 析　xī　analysis

分析　fēnxī　analysis

木＋斤 → 析

"斤"指"斧子",用斧子砍木头,表示分开的意思,后引申为分析、辨析等义。

斤 symbolizes "an axe" that can be used to chop wood. Thus 析 implies "analysis".

析	析											

8 取　qǔ　to get

取得　qǔdé　to get

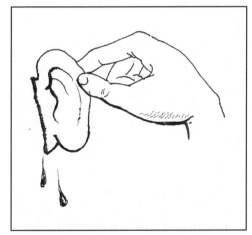

耳＋又 → 取

"耳"指"耳朵","又"是一只手。古字像一只手拿着一只被割下来的耳朵,中国古代战争中以割取敌方耳朵来记功,后引申为拿、获取。

耳 symbolizes an ear, and 又 a human hand. Hence an ear in the hand suggests "obtain". Formerly a soldier was awarded when he returned from the battlefield with an enemy's ear in hand.

取	取											

❾ 烦 fán annoying

麻烦 máfan trouble

火 + 页 → 烦

"页"指"人头",头如火烧,原指热头痛,引申为烦恼、烦躁。

烦, symbolizing fire above a human head, suggests "fever and headache". By extension it has come to mean "annoying" or "agitated".

烦	烦										

❿ 改 gǎi to change

改变 gǎibiàn to change
改正 gǎizhèng to correct

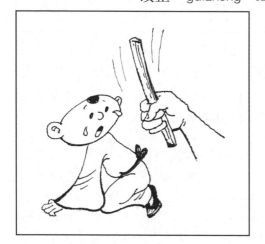

己 + 攵 → 改

古字"己"是孩子的象形,指孩子,"攵"是拿着棍子打。表示责打孩子使之改正错误。

The left component of 改 symbolizes a child, and its right component a stick for beating. The combination of the two suggests "a child corrects himself after a corporal punishment".

改	改	改	改								

⑪ 初 chū beginning

初级 chūjí primary

初中 chūzhōng junior middle school

衣＋刀→初

"衤"指衣服，用刀裁衣，这是制作衣服的开始。

The two components of 初 symbolize cloth and a knife for cutting —— the first step of clothes making.

初	初										

⑫ 解 jiě to understand，to undo

了解 liǎojiě to understand

解决 jiějué to solve, solution

角＋刀＋牛

→解

用刀把牛剖开，后引申为分解、解释等意思。

The character 解 about how an ox is cut off by a knife implies "disintegrate" or "explain".

解	解	解	解	解	解	解	解				

⑬ 鲜　xiān　fresh，delicious

新鲜　xīnxiān　fresh
鲜花　xiānhuā　fresh flowers

鱼＋羊→鲜

鱼肉和羊肉味道很鲜美,以此来代表鲜美的食物。"鲜"的本义是鲜美、新鲜。

Fish and lamb are delicious food. Thus the original meaning of 鲜 is "tasty" or "fresh".

鲜	鲜										

⑭ 位　wèi　seat

座位　zuòwèi　seat
位置　wèizhì　seat，place，position

亻＋立→位

"亻"指"人","立"是站立,人站立需要一个位置。

位 indicates a place where a man stands.

位	位										

15 信 xìn letter，to believe in

信封 xìnfēng envelope
短信 duǎnxìn nofe
相信 xiāngxìn to believe
信心 xìnxīn confidence，faith

亻＋言→信

"亻"指人，"言"指说话，人应该说话算数，这就是守信用。现代汉语里还有"守信""失信"等说法。

信，formed by 亻（a person）and 言（speech），means "keep one's word".

信	信											

16 冰 bīng ice

冰箱 bīngxiāng refrigerator
滑冰 huábīng skating

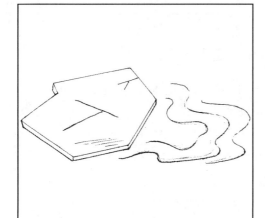

冫＋水→冰

"冫"是冰块破裂后的纹路，水遇冷就结成了冰。

冫 symbolizes the lines on the broken surface of ice made by cold water.

冰	冰	冰	冰	冰								

17 泪　lèi　tear

眼泪　yǎnlèi　tear

$$氵＋目→泪$$

"氵"表示液体,"目"是眼睛,从眼睛里流出的液体就是眼泪。

泪 formed by 氵(liquid) and 目（eyes）means "tears".

泪	泪												

18 汽　qì　steam

汽车　qìchē　automobile
公共汽车　gōnggòng qìchē　bus

$$氵＋气→汽$$

"氵"指水,"气"是气体。由水变成的气体就是水蒸气。

汽 formed by 氵（water）and 气（gas）means "steam".

汽	汽	汽	汽	汽									

⑲ 沙　shā　sand

沙发　shāfā　sofa
沙漠　shāmò　desert

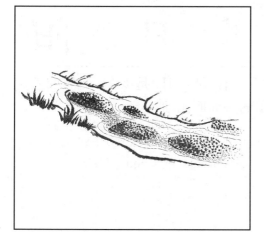

$$氵 + 少 \rightarrow 沙$$

水中的沙石,沉在水底,水少了就可以见到。

Sands and stones can be seen in shallow water.

沙	沙	沙	沙	沙							

⑳ 酒　jiǔ　alcoholic drink

酒吧　jiǔbā　bar
葡萄酒　pútaojiǔ　wine

$$氵 + 酉 \rightarrow 酒$$

"氵"指液体,"酉"是盛酒的器皿,酒具里的液体就是酒。

酒 formed by 氵(liquid) and 酉 (wine container) means "alcoholic drink".

酒	酒	酒	酒	酒	酒	酒	酒				

㉑ 阳 yáng sun

太阳　tàiyáng　sun
阳台　yángtái　balcony

阝＋日 → 阳

"阝"指山坡,"日"是太阳,山坡向着太阳的一面叫阳面。

> 阳 formed by 阝（slope）and 日（the sun）means "the sunny side".

阳	阳												

㉒ 阴 yīn cloudy

阴天　yīntiān　cloudy

阝＋月 → 阴

"阝"指山坡,"月"是月亮,山坡背着阳光的一面就像在月光下一样阴暗。

> 阴 formed by 阝（slope）and 月（the moon）means "as dim as under the moon".

阴	阴												

㉓ 鸣 míng to cry

鸣叫 míngjiào to cry

口 + 鸟 → 鸣

"鸟"用"口"叫,表示鸣叫的意思。

In the character 鸣, a bird and its mouth together suggest "birds' singing".

鸣	鸣	鸣	鸣	鸣	鸣						

㉔ 利 lì benefit, sharp

顺利 shùnlì smooth
利用 lìyòng to use, to make use of
有利 yǒulì beneficial, favourable
流利 liúlì fluent, smooth

禾 + 刂 → 利

"禾"指庄稼,"刂"指刀,用刀割庄稼,谷粒随刀纷纷落下,说明刀是锋利的,刀锋利使用起来就方便,所以"利"引申为顺利、便利的意思。

利 formed by 禾 (crops) and 刂 (knife) depicts the convenience in cutting crops with a sharpened knife.

利	利										

㉕ 删　shān　to delete

删去　shānqu　to delete

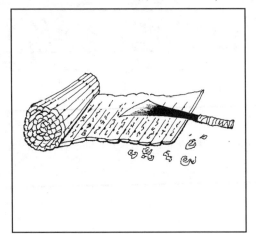

册 ＋ 刂 → 删

"册"是古代用竹简做成的书,"刂"指刀。在古代,要用刀才能把竹简上的字删去。

册 symbolizes an ancient book made of bamboo slips beside a knife. Any deletion on such a book could only be made with a knife.

删 删 删 删 删 删

㉖ 班　bān　shift

上班　shàng bān　to go to work
下班　xià bān　to come off work
班长　bānzhǎng　monitor

王 ＋ 刂 ＋ 王 → 班

"王"指玉,"刂"是刀的变体,指刀。原义是用刀来分玉,后来泛指组织的编排和划分,如"班级"。

In the character 班, 王 symbolizes "jade", 刂 is a variant form of 刀 (knife). Originally the character means "the cutting of jade with a knife", now by extension has come to mean "class".

班 班 班 班

㉗ 粥   zhōu   porridge

小米粥   xiǎomǐ zhōu   millet gruel

$$弓 + 米 + 弓 \rightarrow 粥$$

两个"弓"指强力,用强力(指猛火)才能把米煮烂,熬成稀粥。

Two 弓 (bows) symbolize "powerful". Rice or millet can be cooked only with considerable heat into porridge.

粥	粥	粥											

㉘ 掰   bāi   to break off

掰开   bāikāi   to break off

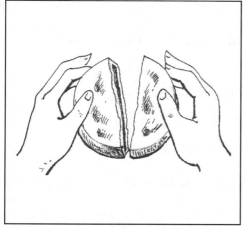

$$手 + 分 + 手 \rightarrow 掰$$

用两手把东西分开就是"掰"。

The character 掰 means "break something off with both hands".

掰	掰	掰	掰										

认读词、词组和句子

Read the Following Words，Phrases and Sentences

一、认读词、词组
Read the Following Words and Phrases.

如：如果　比如　不如　如此　如今　如同　如意

妇：少妇　老妇　农妇　妇科　妇产科　妇科医生

从：从来　从小　从上到下　从明天起　从此
　　从早到晚　从前

双：一双手　一双脚　一双筷子　一双鞋　双方

林：树林　竹林　园林　果林　林业

改：改革　改进　改动　改换　改行　改日　改天
　　改期　改写

初：初级　初步　初中　初学　初次　初冬

鲜：鲜血　鲜肉　鲜鱼　新鲜空气

位：一位老人　一位老师　位子　座位

信：写信　一封信　信纸　信件　贺信　发信　明信片
　　通信　信息　可信　自信

冰：冰箱　冰水　冰凉　冰鞋　冰天雪地

酒：啤酒　红酒　白酒　鸡尾酒　香槟(bīn)酒　酒吧
　　酒店　酒馆　酒杯　酒量

利：不利　利息

班：上班　下班　全班　班级　班长　班车　航班
　　加班

二、认读下列句子
Read the Following Sentences.

1. 我们才认识一个多月，所以我刚开始对他有了一些了解。

2. 树林里虫鸣鸟叫的，很热闹。

3. 我们国家的妇女都工作。夫妇俩都工作，所以有时候就要让老人来帮助照顾孩子。

4. 今天是阴天，没有太阳，所以我睡到九点半才醒。

5. 如果我说错，请告诉我，这样我就可以马上改正。

6. 我们班很多同学学习很努力，比如阿里、夏子、山本等。

7. 不明白她为什么哭了，眼泪都出来了。

8. 那位老人在沙发上睡着了，双手还拿着一张报纸。

9. 同志，这双鞋太小，麻烦你换一双。

10. 你们学校在北京市什么位置？坐公共汽车方便吗？

11. 啤酒太凉了，不如喝一点儿红葡萄酒吧。

12. 这些菜刚从冰箱里拿出来，还很新鲜。

13. 他常常利用下班时间跟留学生练习英语，他现在说得比以前流利多了。

14. 他开着汽车在那片沙漠里走了两天才走出来。

15. 今天请大家来是想让大家一起商量一下解决交通问题的方法。

16. 通过一年的学习，你们取得了很大的成绩。

17. 我不相信这个人，你们也很难改变我对他的看法。

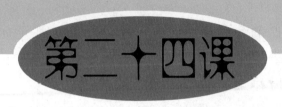

基本知识
Rudiments of Chinese Characters

汉字的书写(五)
The writing of Chinese Characters（E）

合体字的书写,要分清字的结构形式,要注意结构之间大小、宽窄的变化,还要注意或高或低、或长或短的位置安排。一般来说,笔画多,所占位置大,笔画少,所占位置小。

In writing combined characters one shoulld pay attention to their structure, gap in between, height, length, and position in between. Generally speaking those characters formed by more strokes are of bigger size, whereas those by fewer strokes are of smaller size.

左右结构：

Characters in a left-and-right structure：

鲜	明	醉	左右相等	equal sized components on both sides
刻	彩	都	左大右小	a bigger sized component on the left than the one on the right
快	现	睡	左小右大	a smaller sized component on the left than the one on the right

喝	嘴	峰	右面略高 a higher placed component on the right than the one on the left
知	和	叔	右面略低 a lower placed component on the right than the one on the left

上下结构：

Characters in an up-and-down structure：

志	留	男	上下相等 equal sized components both on the top and underneath
您	照	雪	上大下小 a bigger sized component on the top than the one underneath
字	筷	最	上小下大 a smaller sized component on the top than the one underneath

包围结构：

Characters in an encircling structure：

度	越	句	两包围要包得住 well contained in its two-sided closing formation
风	同	向	上包围，被包围部分稍向上框靠 placed higher in its up closing formation
凶	击	画	下包围，被包围部分稍向下框靠 placed lower in its low closing formation
区	匹	医	左包围，被包围部分稍向左边靠 placed on the left in its left closing formation
回	国	园	全包围，框内空间应饱满、均匀 well and proportionally contained in its fully encircling formation

生字词表
List of New Characters and Words

1.	男	nán	man
	男人	nánrén	man
	男朋友	nán péngyou	boyfriend
2.	旦	dàn	dawn
	元旦	yuándàn	New Year's Day
3.	旱	hàn	dry
	干旱	gānhàn	dry
4.	美	měi	beautiful, very satisfactory
	美元	měiyuán	U. S. dollar
	美好	měihǎo	happy, bright
	美容	měiróng	hairdressing
5.	尖	jiān	pointed
	尖刀	jiāndāo	sharp knife
6.	尘	chén	dust
	尘土	chéntǔ	dust
	吸尘器	xīchénqì	vacuum cleaner
7.	至	zhì	to
	至少	zhìshǎo	at least
	至今	zhìjīn	up to now
	至于	zhìyú	as to
8.	合	hé	to combine
	合适	héshì	suitable
	合同	hétóng	contract
	合作	hézuò	to cooperate
9.	友	yǒu	friend
	朋友	péngyou	friend
	女朋友	nǔ péngyou	girlfriend

	友好	yǒuhǎo	friendly
10.	灰	huī	dust
	灰尘	huīchén	dust
	灰色	huīsè	grey
11.	灭	miè	to put out
	灭火	miè huǒ	to put out a fire
12.	灾	zāi	disaster
	火灾	huǒzāi	fire
13.	炎	yán	scorching
	炎热	yánrè	scorching
14.	室	shì	room
	卧室	wòshì	bedroom
	浴室	yùshì	bathroom
	聊天室	liáotiānshì	chat room
15.	宝	bǎo	treasure
	宝贵	bǎoguì	precious
16.	盲	máng	blind
	盲人	mángrén	blind man
17.	采	cǎi	to pick up
	采访	cǎifǎng	to cover
	采取	cǎiqǔ	to adopt，to take
18.	光	guāng	light
	阳光	yángguāng	sunshine
19.	歪	wāi	askew
	帽子歪了	màozi wāi le	This cap is not erect.
20.	甭	béng	don't, needn't
21.	臭	chòu	smelly
22.	岩	yán	rock
	岩石	yánshí	rock
23.	弄	nòng	to make

弄错	nòngcuò	to make a mistake
弄清	nòngqīng	to make clear
24. 套	tào	set, cover, (a measure word)
外套	wàitào	outer garment
手套	shǒutào	gloves
25. 您	nín	you
您好	nín hǎo	How do you do?
26. 黑	hēi	black
黑色	hēisè	black
黑白	hēibái	black and white
27. 墨	mò	ink
墨水	mòshuǐ	ink
28. 众	zhòng	multitude
众多	zhòngduō	numerous
观众	guānzhòng	audience
听众	tīngzhòng	audience
29. 森	sēn	forest
森林	sēnlín	forest
30. 品	pǐn	item, product
商品	shāngpǐn	goods
食品	shípǐn	food
日用品	rìyòngpǐn	basic commodities
产品	chǎnpǐn	product
31. 晶	jīng	crystalline
亮晶晶	liàngjīngjīng	shiny
32. 国	guó	country
国家	guójiā	country
国籍	guójí	nationality
国内	guónèi	internal, domestic
国外	guówài	external, overseas

	国际	guójì	international
33.	内	nèi	inside
	内容	nèiróng	content
34.	库	kù	storehouse
	车库	chēkù	garage
35.	尾	wěi	tail
	尾巴	wěiba	tail
	结尾	jiéwěi	ending

汉字的笔画和生字的书写
The Strokes and Writing of the New Characters

会意字
Associative Characters

① 男 nán man

男人 nánrén man

男朋友 nán péngyou boyfriend

田 + 力 → 男

"田"是田地,"力"是力气。在田里劳动的是男子,因为他们有力气。

男 is composed of 田 (farmland) and 力 (strength). A man works in the fields because he is strong.

男	男											

2 旦 dàn dawn

元旦 yuándàn New Year's Day

"日"是太阳,下面的一横表示地平线,太阳刚从地平线上升起,表示天亮、早晨的意思。

旦 is composed of 日（the sun）and 一（the horizon）. Their combined meaning is "early morning when the sun is above the horizon".

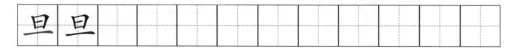

3 旱 hàn dry

干旱 gānhàn dry

"日"是太阳,"干"是干燥,天旱的时候,太阳炎热,天气干燥。

旱 is composed of 日（the sun）and 干（dry）. Their combined meaning is "dry weather caused by the scorching sun".

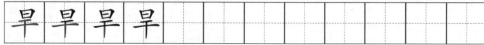

4 美　měi　beautiful，very satisfactory

美元　měiyuán　U. S. dollar
美好　měihǎo　happy，bright
美容　měiróng　hairdressing

羊 十 大 → 美

在几种主要的家畜中,肥大的羊肉味最鲜美。"美"的本义是"味道好",后引申为美好、美丽等义。

Of many domestic animals fat sheep is delicious food. The original meaning of 美 is "tasty", by extension it has come to mean "beautiful".

美　美　美

5 尖　jiān　pointed

尖刀　jiāndāo　sharp knife

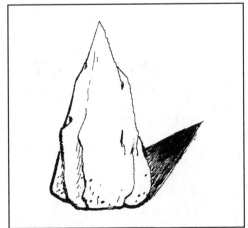

小 十 大 → 尖

上面小,下面大,这是尖的形状。

尖 means anything with a fine cutting end.

尖　尖

6 尘　　chén　dust

尘土　chéntǔ　dust

吸尘器　xīchénqì　vacuum cleaner

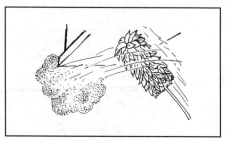 

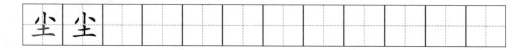

灰尘就是小的土。"尘"的繁体为"塵",是鹿跑的时候身后扬起的土。

尘 means the fine powder of dry earth.

尘	尘										

7 至　　zhì　to

至少　zhìshǎo　at least

至今　zhìjīn　up to now

至于　zhìyú　as to

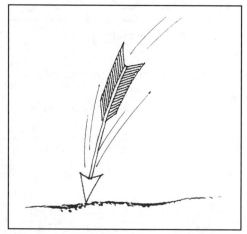

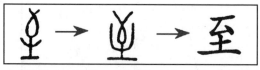

古字形上面是一支箭,下面的一横是箭射到的地方,表示到达的意思,后引申为"极"义。

The ancient written form of 至 is in the shape of an arrow upon a target indicated by a horizontal stroke. Originally the character meant "arrive", by extension it has come to mean "extreme".

至	至	至									

8 合　hé　to combine

合适　héshì　suitable
合同　hétóng　contract
合作　hézuò　to cooperate

"亼"指器皿的盖儿，在器皿上加盖儿，上下口儿就相合了。

合 is formed by 亼 (a container) and a lid.

合	合	合										

9 友　yǒu　friend

朋友　　péngyou　friend
女朋友　nǚ péngyou　girlfriend
友好　　yǒuhǎo　friendly

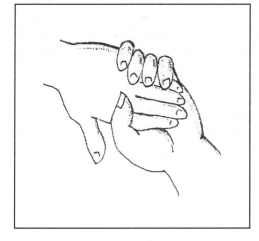

"ナ"和"又"在古汉字中都表示手，"ナ"表示左手，"又"表示右手，两只手握在一起是为了表示友好。

Both components（ナ and 又）of 友 meant "hand" in classical Chinese. The shaking of two hands expresses "friendship".

友	友											

❿ 灰 huī dust

灰尘 huīchén dust
灰色 huīsè grey

ナ ＋ 火 ━▶ 灰

"ナ"是一只手,用手把火熄灭后,剩下的就是灰了。

ナ of 灰 symbolizes "a hand". What is expressed here is the ashes after a fire is put out by a hand.

灰	灰	灰	灰	灰	灰							

⓫ 灭 miè to put out

灭火 miè huǒ to put out a fire

一 ＋ 火 ━▶ 灭

"火"指"火焰","一"表示在火上盖压东西,这样火就灭了。

灭 is in the shape of flames put out by something spread over.

灭	灭	灭	灭	灭								

⑫ 灾　zāi　disaster

火灾　huǒzāi　fire

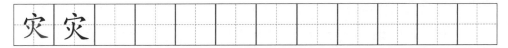

"宀"是房屋，屋里失火就是一种灾难，后来其他原因引起的祸害也称为灾，如水灾等。

The top component of 灾 symbolizes "a house" where there is a disaster caused by a fire inside. By extension it has come to mean any terrible misfortune.

灾	灾												

⑬ 炎　yán　scorching

炎热　yánrè　scorching

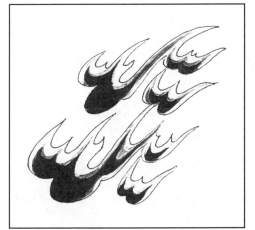

上下两个火字，火上加火，表示焚烧之烈，火势很大，温度自然就高了。

炎 in the form of double fires means "extremely hot".

炎	炎												

⑭ 室 shì room

卧室　wòshì　bedroom
浴室　yùshì　bothroom
聊天室　liáotiānshì　chat room

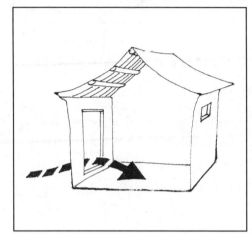

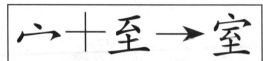

"宀"指屋子，"至"是"到"的意思，到了屋子里边就进入了"室"内。

室 formed by 宀（a house）and 至（arrive）means "a place where one enters".

室	室								

⑮ 宝 bǎo treasure

宝贵　bǎoguì　precious

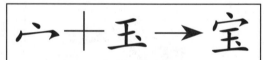

"宀"是屋子。"玉"指玉石，家里珍藏的玉石等是宝贵的东西。

宝 formed by 宀（a house）and 玉（jade）means "treasure".

宝	宝								

16 盲　máng　blind

盲人　mángrén　blind man

亡 + 目 → 盲

"亡"是"无",即没有,眼中无眸表示眼睛看不见。

盲 formed by 亡（nothing）and 目（eyes）means "see nothing".

盲	盲	盲	盲								

17 采　cǎi　to pick up

采访　cǎifǎng　to cover

采取　cǎiqǔ　to adopt, to take

爫 + 木 → 采

"爫"指一只手,一只手正在采摘树上的果实。

采 depicts how a human hand is picking fruit from a tree.

采	采	采	采	采							

⑱ 光 guāng light

阳光 yángguāng sunshine

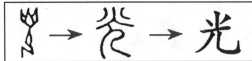

古字形像一个跪坐着的人,头上是"火"字,表示火能够给人们带来光明。

The ancient written form of 光 is in the shape of a man sitting on his knees under a light.

光	光	光	光	光	光									

⑲ 歪 wāi askew

房子歪了 fángzi wāi le

This house is not erect.

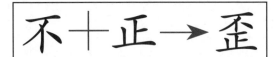

不正就是歪。

歪 means 不 (not) and 正 (erect position).

歪	歪	歪	歪	歪	歪	歪	歪	歪				

20 甭　béng　don't，needn't

不用就是甭。

甭　formed by 不（not）and 用（need）means "needn't".

| 甭 | 甭 | 甭 | 甭 | 甭 | 甭 | 甭 | 甭 | 甭 | | | |

21 臭　chòu　smelly

自 ＋ 犬 → 臭

"自"是鼻子，象形字"自"见上册第 64 页，"犬"是狗，本义是狗用鼻子闻其他禽的气味，后引申为臭气。

臭　formed by 自（a nose）and 犬（a dog）means "a dog smells something out". By extension it has come to mean "a bad smell".

| 臭 | 臭 | 臭 | 臭 | 臭 | 臭 | 臭 | 臭 | 臭 | 臭 | | |

22 岩　yán　rock
　　岩石　yánshí　rock

山 ＋ 石 → 岩

山上的石头就是岩石。

岩（cliff）is a rock in the mountain.

| 岩 | 岩 | 岩 | 岩 | 岩 | 岩 | | | | | | |

㉓ 弄 nòng　to make

弄错　nòngcuò　to make a mistake
弄清　nòngqīng　to make clear

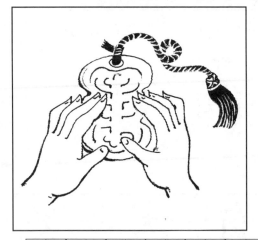

王 ＋ 廾 → 弄

古字形像双手捧着玉。上面的"王"指玉，玉是常用做玩赏的珍品，下面的"廾"表示两只手，表示"玩弄"的意思。

The ancient written form of 弄 is in the shape of a piece of jade held by two hands. The character means "play with".

弄 弄 弄 弄

㉔ 套 tào　set, cover, (a measure word)

外套　wàitào　outer garment
手套　shǒutào　gloves

大 ＋ 镸 → 套

"镸"是"长"的另一种写法。"长"是"镸"的简体。大一点，长一点，才能套上被套的物件。后引申指同类事物的一组，如"一套衣服""一套家具"等。

镸 is another written form of 长, or simplified 镸. Bigger things can hold smaller ones. Hence 套 is used as a measure word in the sense of "suit" for clothes or of "set" for furniture.

套 套 套 套 套 套 套 套

㉕ 您 nín you

您好 nín hǎo How do you do?

你 十 心 → 您

心中的"你"就是"您"，"您"为敬称。

您 is in the form of "you" in a human heart, hence it is used as a polite form of "you".

| 您 | 您 | 您 | 您 | 您 | 您 | 您 | 您 | 您 | | |

㉖ 黑 hēi black

黑色 hēisè black
黑白 hēibái black and white

古字形上面是"囱"，表示烟囱，下面是"炎"，燃烧后的烟从烟囱冒出去，经过的地方颜色就变黑了。

The ancient written form of 黑 is in the shape of a chimney above double fires, Figuratively 黑（black）is the colour resulted from the smoke out of a chimney.

| 黑 | 黑 | 黑 | 黑 | 黑 | 黑 | 黑 | 黑 | | | | |

27 墨　　mò　ink

墨水　mòshuǐ　ink

黑 ＋ 土 → 墨

中国人写毛笔字或作画时用的墨是用一种黑色的土研磨而成的。

The ink used for Chinese writing and painting is traditionally made of powdered black earth.

墨	墨									

28 众　　zhòng　multitude

众多　zhòngduō　numerous
观众　guānzhòng　audience
听众　tīngzhòng　audience

人 ＋ 人 ＋ 人 → 众

三个人站立在一起，表示人很多，人多即为"众"。这种把两个或三个同样的事物放在一起来表示数量多的构字法还有"林""多""品""森"等字。

Three people standing together symbolize "multitude". Similar examples are 林, 多, 品 and 森.

众	众	众								

29 森　sēn　forest

森林　sēnlín　forest

木 ＋ 木 ＋ 木
→ 森

三个"木"表示树很多很多,有很多很多树的地方就是森林了。

Three trees growing together symbolize "a forest".

森	森	森										

30 品　pǐn　item, product

商品　shāngpǐn　goods
食品　shípǐn　food
日用品　rìyòngpǐn　basic commodities
产品　chǎnpǐn　product

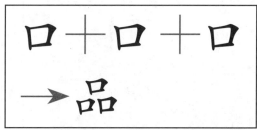

口 ＋ 口 ＋ 口
→ 品

"口"指器皿,三个器皿放在一起表示品类很多。

Three containers put together symbolize "all types of items".

品	品	品										

31 晶　jīng　crystalline

亮晶晶　liàngjīngjīng　shiny

日十日十日
→ 晶

"日"在这里指星星，三颗星星表示多，很多星星在一起表示晶莹明净的意思。

Here 日 stands for a star. Three stars twinkling together symbolize "crystalline".

晶	晶	晶										

32 国　guó　country

国家　guójiā　country
国籍　guójí　nationality
国内　guónèi　internal, domestic
国外　guówài　external, overseas
国际　guójì　international

口十或十國
→ 国

"或"表示以"戈"（武器）守卫"口"（城邑），外面加一方框表示疆域，合在一起就是国家的意思。"國"是繁体。

The complicated form of 國 consists of 戈 (dagger-axe) and 口 (walled-city). The components together express the meaning of "country". 国 is the simplified form of 國.

国	国	国	国									

③③ 内 nèi inside

内容 nièróng content

冂 十 人 → 内

"冂"表示一定的范围,进入里边就是
到了这个范围"内"。

The character depicts what is put in a place, meaning "inside".

内	内	内										

③④ 库 kù storehouse

车库 chēkù garage

广 十 车 → 库

"广"指房屋,存放战车的房屋就是
"库",后泛指贮藏东西的房屋或地方。

广 stands for house. 库 is a storehouse where war chariots are parked. The two components together mean "storehouse".

库	库											

35 尾　wěi　tail

尾巴　wěiba　tail
结尾　jiéwěi　ending

尸＋毛→尾

"尸"表示人的躯体,古字形像一个人的臀部系一条尾巴状的饰物。本义指动物的尾巴,后引申为末尾、后面的意思。

尸 stands for a human body. The ancient written form of 尾 is in the shape of a man with something like a tail. Originally the character meant "tail", by extension it has come to mean "end" or "back".

尾	尾	尾	尾	尾								

认读词、词组和句子
Read the Following Words，Phrases and Sentences

一、认读词、词组
Read the Following Words and Phrases.

男：男人　男朋友　男孩子　男子　男子汉　男生
　　男女　男厕(cè)所
美：美元　美国　美好　美女　美梦　美满　美人
　　美化　美酒　美容院
尘：沙尘　尘烟

至：至多　至少

合：合同　合作　合唱　集合　合影　合法　合理

友：友好　校友　亲友　友爱　友情　友人　好友
　　老友　交朋友

灰：灰色　灰白　灰心　烟灰　纸灰

灾：火灾　水灾　灾区　灾民　灾难　灾情　天灾

室：教室　休息室　会客室　地下室　办公室　候车室
　　室内　室外

宝：宝石　宝玉　宝贝　宝物　宝库　国宝　红宝石
　　蓝宝石

光：灯光　火光　目光　月光　星光　光滑　光明

套：一套衣服　一套房子　一套沙发　一套家具

黑：黑板　黑色　天黑　黑心　黑龙江

众：众人　大众　公众　民众

品：食品　商品　礼品　作品　品种　甜品　工业品
　　农产品

国：国家　全国　各国　国内　国外　国歌　国旗
　　国庆节　国情　爱国　出国　回国　外国　邻国

内：内衣　校内　室内　国内　市内　城内　内心
　　内部

库：宝库　国库　金库　冷库　书库　水库　血库

二、认读下列句子

Read the Following Sentences.

1. 在我们国家,这种水果大概五美元一斤。

2. 电影的结尾太感人(moving)了,很多观众流下了眼泪。

3. 他在采访一位灰白头发的老人。

4. 因为天气炎热、气候干旱,那片森林上个月发生了火
   灾,现在火灭了。

5. 那个商店的商品品种很多,有各种各样的食品和日用品。

6. 这件灰色的外套很合适,也很好看。

7. 那座山上的岩石很多。

8. 我那双黑色的手套不见了。

9. 篮球场在车库的南边。

10. 吸尘器坏了,这个星期没有收拾房间,到处都是灰尘。

11. 这个鸡蛋臭了。

12. 这套房子有两个卧室,还有厨房、客厅、浴室和一个阳台,特别是两个卧室都在阳面,冬天阳光很好。

13. 甭着急,先把情况弄清楚,再想应该采取什么办法来解决。

14. 至今,灾区人民得到了国际国内众多有爱心的人们的热情帮助。

15. 合同的内容没有什么问题。来,为我们双方的友好合作干杯。

第二十五课

基本知识
Rudiments of Chinese Characters

汉字的造字方法（四）
The Formation of Chinese Characters（D）

形声字
Pictophonetic Characters

由表意的形旁和表音的声旁两部分构成的合体字叫形声字。如：

> Pictophonetic characters are composed of a pictographic component and a phonetic component. For example：

女（形旁）＋马（声旁）→妈（形声字）

> The pictogrophic component The phonetic component Pictophonetic characte

在现代汉字中，90％左右的合体字是形声字。前面我们已经学过，形声字的形旁表示字的意义类属，它能帮助我们了解该字意义的大致范围，可以帮助我们记忆和掌握字形和字义。

> Pictophonetic characters amount to 90 per cent of the total modern Chinese characters. The pictographic components of such character indicate their significance in general，are helpful for learners to memorize and have a good command of their strokes and meaning.

形声字的声旁对字的读音具有一定的提示作用,我们把形声字的声旁和这个汉字的读音关系分为以下几类:

The phonetic components of such character indicate their pronunciation as a general rule. They function in the following ways:

1. 声旁的读音与字音完全相同,如:

The phonetic component shows the right pronunciation of the character it belongs to, for example:

元(yuán)——园(yuán)　　哥(gē)——歌(gē)

2. 声旁的读音与字音声韵相同,声调不同,如:

The phonetic component shows the right phonetic elements of the character with a different tone, for example:

方(fāng)——房(fáng)　访(fǎng)　放(fàng)
巴(bā)——吧(ba)　　把(bǎ)　　爸(bà)

3. 声旁的读音与字音声母相同,韵母不同,如:

The phonetic component indicates the right initial but different final of the syllable that the character stands for, for example

先(xiān)——洗(xǐ)　　母(mǔ)——每(měi)

4. 声旁的读音与字音韵母相同,声母不同,如:

The phonetic component indicates the right final but different initial of the syllable that the character stands for, for example:

齐(qí)——挤(jǐ)　　济(jì)
门(mén)——问(wèn)　闻(wén)

5. 声旁的读音与字音声母、韵母都不同,如:

The phonetic component indicates a syllable of which the initial and final are different from what the character stands for, for example:

半(bàn)——胖(pàng)　　果(guǒ)——课(kè)

在现代汉字中,有一些形声字的声旁已经完全失去了表音功能,所以对大多数汉字,我们还是要通过汉语拼音来掌握它们的正确读音。

Of the modern Chinese characters some phonetic components do not indicate the right pronunciation of the characters they belong to. It is advisable for students to have a good command of the pronunciation of the characters by learning their corresponding phonetically alphabetic writing.

生字词表
List of New Characters and Words

1. 冒	mào	to take risks
感冒	gǎnmào	to have a cold
2. 介	jiè	to be situated between
介绍	jièshào	to introduce
3. 平	píng	calm, smooth, level
水平	shuǐpíng	level
平时	píngshí	as usual
4. 苹	píng	
苹果	píngguǒ	apple
5. 谊	yì	friendship
友谊	yǒuyì	friendship
6. 菜	cài	dish
菜谱	càipǔ	menu
点菜	diǎn cài	to order food
白菜	báicài	chinese cabbage
蔬菜	shūcài	vegetables
7. 录	lù	to copy, to record
录音	lùyīn	to record, to tape
8. 适	shì	to suit
适应	shìyìng	to suit, to adapt

9. 讲	jiǎng	to say
讲话	jiǎnghuà	to speak，speech
10. 济	jì	to help
经济	jīngjì	economy
11. 齐	qí	neat，together
一齐	yìqí	all of a lump
12. 给	gěi	to give
13. 升	shēng	to move upward，to promote
上升	shàngshēng	to rise
14. 便	①biàn	convenience
方便	fāngbiàn	convenience
	②pián	
便宜	piányi	cheap
15. 使	shǐ	to make，to enable，messenger
大使馆	dàshǐguǎn	embassy
使用	shǐyòng	to use
16. 直	zhí	straight
一直	yìzhí	straight，continuously
17. 具	jù	to possess，tool
工具	gōngjù	tool
玩具	wánjù	toy
真	zhēn	real
真正	zhēnzhèng	really
18. 堂	táng	hall
教堂	jiàotáng	church
19. 经	jīng	to pass through，to stand
经常	jīngcháng	often
经过	jīngguò	to pass，as a result，process
经理	jīnglǐ	manager，conductor

20.	渴	kě	thirsty
	口渴	kǒu kě	thirsty
21.	蓝	lán	blue
	蓝色	lánsè	blue
22.	寓	yù	residence
	公寓	gōngyù	apartment house
23.	牌	pái	plate, brand, card
	牌子	páizi	brand, sign
	名牌	míngpái	famous brand
	打牌	dǎ pái	play cards
24.	版	bǎn	edition
	出版	chūbǎn	to publish
25.	播	bō	to broadcast
	广播	guǎngbō	to broadcast
26.	蛋	dàn	egg
	蛋糕	dàngāo	cake
	笨蛋	bèndàn	fool, idiot
27.	楚	chǔ	clear
	清楚	qīngchu	clear
28.	绍	shào	(short form for Shaoxing, Zhejiang Province)
	介绍	jièshào	to introduce
29.	橘	jú	tangerine
	橘子	júzi	tangerine
30.	世	shì	age, world
	世纪	shìjì	century
31.	表	biǎo	watch, form, to express
	手表	shǒubiǎo	wrist watch
32.	戴	dài	to wear, to put on
	戴上帽子	dàishang màozi	to put on one's hat

33. 瓶	píng	bottle
瓶子	píngzi	bottle
34. 舒	shū	to stretch
舒服	shūfu	comfortable
35. 嘴	zuǐ	mouth
嘴巴	zuǐba	mouth
36. 鼻	bí	nose
鼻子	bízi	nose
37. 重	zhòng	heavy, serious, weight
重要	zhòngyào	important
重视	zhòngshì	to attach importance to
38. 最	zuì	most
最后	zuìhòu	final
最初	zuìchū	initial, first
最好	zuìhǎo	best, had better
最多	zuìduō	most, at most
39. 事	shì	affair, matter, trouble
事情	shìqíng	affair, thing, business
办事	bànshì	to handle affairs
事先	shìxiān	in advance
同事	tóngshì	fellow worker
40. 当	dāng	when, to serve as
当然	dānrán	of course
当 ...... 的时候	dāng… de shíhou	when..., at the time...
41. 需	xū	to need, to require
需要	xūyào	to need, to require, needs

生字的比较和书写

The Comparison and Writing of the New Characters

一、对比下列各组例字,注意分析下列各组声旁字与由该声旁字组成的汉字,
两者之间的读音有什么关系。(汉字前有＊号的为已学过的汉字,请在其
后边的括号内写出它们的拼音和组词,并画出其中生字的字形结构图)

例:(一)哥(gē)—歌(gē)

帽—冒

＊帽(mào)(帽子)

① 冒　　mào　to take risks

感冒　gǎnmào　to have a cold

1	
2	

①曰　②目

介—界 { 界—介
＊界(　　) (　　)

② 介　　jiè　to be situated between

介绍　jièshào　to introduce

平—苹 { 苹—平
＊苹(　　) (　　)

③ 平　　píng　calm, smooth, level

水平　shuǐpíng　level

平时　píngshí　as usual

(二)方(　　)—放(　　)

谊—宜

＊谊(　　) (　　)

④ 谊　　yì　friendship

友谊　yǒuyì　friendship

☐

采—菜
＊采(　　)　(　　)

5 菜　cài　dish

☐

菜谱　càipǔ　menu
点菜　diǎn cài　to order food
白菜　báicài　Chinese cabbage
蔬菜　shūcài　vegetables

(三)母(　　)—每(　　)

绿—录
＊绿(　　)　(　　)

6 录　lù　to copy, to record

☐

录音　lùyīn　to record, to tape

舌—适
＊舌(　　)　(　　)

7 适　shì　to suit

☐

适应　shìyìng　to suit, to adapt

井—讲
＊井(　　)　(　　)

8 讲　jiǎng　to say

☐

讲话　jiǎnghuà　to speak, speech

(四)门(   )一问(   )

    挤—济—齐

    ＊挤(   )(   )

⑨ 济   jì to help

        经济 jīngjì economy

☐

⑩ 齐   qí neat，together

        一齐 yìqí all of a lump

☐

(五)半(   )一胖(   )

    合—给

    ＊合(   )(   )

⑪ 给   gěi to give

☐

二、比较下列各组形近字

    （加"＊"的汉字已经学过,请在其后的括号内写出它们的拼音和组词,并画出其中的生字的字形结构图）

(一)开—井—升

    ＊开(   )(   )

    ＊井(   )(   )

⑫ 升   shēng   to move upward，to promote

        上升 shàngshēng to rise

☐

(二)便—使

⑬ 便   ①biàn convenience

207

□

方便　fāngbiàn　convenience

②pián

便宜　piányi　cheap

⑭ 使

shǐ　to make, to enable, messenger

□

大使馆　dàshǐguǎn　embassy

使用　shǐyòng　to use

(三)真—直—具

＊真(　　)　(　　)

⑮ 直

zhí　straight

□

一直　yìzhí　straight, continuously

⑯ 具

jù　to possess, tool

□

工具　gōngjù　tool

玩具　wánjù　toy

(四)常—堂

＊常(　　)　(　　)

⑰ 堂

táng　hall

□

教堂　jiàotáng　church

(五)轻—经

＊轻(　　)　(　　)

⑱ 经

jīng　to pass through, to stand

□

经常　jīngcháng　often

经过　jīngguò　to pass, as a result, process

经理　jīnglǐ　manager, conductor

（六）喝—渴

　　＊喝（　　）　（　　）

19 渴　　kě　thirsty

　　　　　口渴　kǒu kě　thirsty

（七）篮—蓝

　　＊篮（　　）　（　　）

20 蓝　　lán　blue

　　　　　蓝色　lánsè　blue

（八）遇—寓

　　＊遇（　　）　（　　）

21 寓　　yù　residence

　　　　　公寓　gōngyù　apartment house

（九）啤—牌

　　＊啤（　　）　（　　）

22 牌　　pái　plate, brand, card

　　　　　牌子　páizi　brand, sign
　　　　　名牌　míngpái　famous brand
　　　　　打牌　dǎ pái　play cards

（十）板—版

　　＊板（　　）　（　　）

23 版　　bǎn　edition

　　　　　出版　chūbǎn　to publish

(十一)翻—播

＊翻（　　）　（　　　）

24 播　　bō　to broadcast

广播　guǎngbō　to broadcast

（十二）蛋—楚

25 蛋　　dàn　egg

蛋糕　dàngāo　cake

笨蛋　bèndàn　fool, idiot

26 楚　　chǔ　clear

清楚　qīngchu　clear

(十三)照—绍

＊照（　　）　（　　　）

27 绍　　shào　（short form for Shaoxing, Zhejiang priovince）

介绍　jièshào　to introduce

三、仿照例字,画出下列汉字的字形结构图,并写出它们的笔画顺序。

例 橘　　jú　tangerine

橘子　júzi　tangerine

①木 ②矛 ｜ コ ヌ 予 矛

③冏 ｜ 冂 冂 冏 冏 冏 冏

28 世　　shì　age, world

世纪　shìjì　century

㉙ **表** biǎo   watch, form, to express

手表 shǒubiǎo   wrist watch

☐

㉚ **戴** dài   to wear, to put on

戴上帽子 dàishang màozi   to put on one's hat

☐

㉛ **瓶** píng   bottle

瓶子 píngzi   bottle

☐

㉜ **舒** shū   to stretch

舒服 shūfu   comfortable

☐

㉝ **嘴** zuǐ   mouth

嘴巴 zuǐba   mouth

☐

㉞ **鼻** bí   nose

鼻子 bízi   nose

☐

㉟ **重** zhòng   heavy, serious, weight

重要 zhòngyào   important

重视 zhòngshì   to attach importance to

☐

36 最　zuì　most

最后　zuìhòu　final
最初　zuìchū　initial，first
最好　zuìhǎo　best，had better
最多　zuìduō　most，at most

37 事　shì　affair，matter，trouble

事情　shìqíng　affair，thing，business
办事　bàn shì　to handle affairs
事先　shìxiān　in advance
同事　tóngshì　fellow worker

38 当　dāng　when，to serve as

当然　dāngrán　of course
当……的时候　dāng…de shíhou　when...，at the time...

39 需　xū　to need，to require

需要　xūyào　to need，to require，needs

认读词、词组和句子
Read the Following Words，Phrases and Sentences

一、认读词、词组
Read the Following Words and Phrases.

平：平常　平等　平民　平分　平方米
菜：菜场　菜市　菜地　菜园　菜刀　凉菜　香菜
　　菜花
讲：讲解　讲师　听讲　讲一讲

具：具有 具备 茶具 刀具 灯具 家具 教具 农具 玩具 文具 用具

堂：食堂 礼堂 课堂 天堂

经：已经 经过 经历 经费 经济

牌：一块牌子 汽车牌照 金牌 铜(tóng)牌 银牌 门牌 冒牌 一张牌

蛋：鸡蛋 鸭蛋 鹅蛋 鸟蛋 笨蛋 坏蛋

世：世界 世上 世人 世事 出世 去世 今世 来世 后世

表：表示 表演 表明 钟表 一块表 表哥 表弟 表姐 表妹

瓶：花瓶 暖瓶 一瓶啤酒 一瓶矿泉水

重：重量 轻重 加重 体重 重病 重大 重点 重音

事：有事 好事 坏事 急事 难事 喜事 事假 事件

二、认读下列句子
Read the Following Sentences.

1. 我给你们介绍一下，这位是我的同事，马先生。

2. 他今天感冒了，鼻子不通，所以不去大使馆了。

3. 我一直不太适应这儿的天气，嗓子经常不舒服。

4. 今天是他同屋生日，他给他同屋买了一个蛋糕，还买回来了几瓶啤酒。

5. 最近张经理还出版了一本小说。

6. 我们现在都住在学生公寓，那儿房租比较便宜。

7. 这是菜谱，请问现在需要点菜吗？

8. 这些教学工具不错，使用起来很方便。

9. 他经常把中文广播录下来，然后慢慢地听录音。

10. 经过半年多的努力，他的学习成绩在慢慢上升，汉语水平一天比一天提高了。

11. 这件事很重要，大家都应该重视。

12. 便宜的东西当然就比较容易坏，你看这块手表，刚戴了两个月就坏了。

13. 我平时不喜欢喝水，口渴了才想喝，这个习惯很不好。

14. 你这些东西太重了，飞机上最多只能带 20 公斤。

15. 这些衣服都是国际名牌，当然很贵了。

16. 小平的妈妈常对他说："当大人讲话的时候，小孩子不要随便插(chā)嘴(interrupt)。

17. 我今天下午有事，不能跟你们打牌了。

18. 最近他们国家经济情况不太好，所以不太容易找到好的工作。

附录1

《汉字识写课本》主要部首构字表

二画

厂:历 原 厅

ナ:有 右 友 左 布 灰

匚:医 匹 区

刂(刀):刚 别 到 刮 刻 删 切 分 初

⺈:色 兔 象 急

冂:内 肉 同 网 周

亻:什 们 他 休 体 作 你 位 使 便 信 候 假 化 件 但 住 借 健 俩

人:个 从 今 以 全 会 合 舍 金 众 介

⺈:每 复 午 气 年 舞

八(丷):分 公 共 兴 典 只 具 关 真 黄 弟 单 前 首 半

勹:包 句 勺

儿:元 光 先

亠:六 市 交 高 离 旁 商 就 京

冫:次 冷 净 凉 准 冰 决 况 冬 寒

冖:军 冠 写

讠:认 访 词 试 话 读 译 语 说 请 课 该 谁 谢 让 记 讲 诉 谈 识 谊

阝(左耳):阳 阴 附 院 随 阿

阝(右耳):那 哪 邮 都 部

力:办 加 动 助 努 历 务 男

廴:建 延

又:友 支 双 对 发 观 欢 取 鸡 难

三画

工:左 功 巧

士:声 志 喜

土:去 在 坐 地 场 块 坏 城 址 墨 至 堂 尘

扌:打 找 报 挤 换 操 播 把 接 搬 擦

艹:花 英 草 茶 菜 蓝 苹 蕉

大:太 美 套

⺌:少 堂 常 当 尖 尘

囗:四 因 回 园 国 图 围 圆

口:右 号 只 叫 吃 吗 吧 呢 员 告 听 咳 哪 唱 喝 嗽 和 名 句 各 知 咖 啡 啤 嘴 鸣

巾:布 帮 带 帽 币 市 师 常

山:岁 岩

彳:行 往 很 得 街

彡:须 彩 影 参

犬（犭）：哭 臭 猪 猜 狗
夕：外 名 多 岁 梦
夂：处 冬 务 各 条 备 夏 复
饣：饭 饱 饿 馆 餐 饮 饺
广：床 应 店 度 座 康 库
门：问 间 闻 闹 阅
氵：汉 江 汽 没 法 济 酒 海 渴 游 演 澡 泪 注 泳 法 洗 河 湖 清 满 温 漂
忄：忙 快 惯 慢 怪 情 懂
宀：安 字 完 定 宜 室 家 宿 寒 赛 灾 寓 宝
辶：边 过 进 远 还 近 这 适 迎 送 通 遇 遍
尸：层 局 展 居 尾 屋
弓：张 弯 粥
子：学 孩 孙
女：奶 如 她 好 妈 妹 姐 姓 始 要 妻 妇
纟：红 级 纸 练 绍 经 给 绿
马：驾 骑

四画

王：玩 现 班 球 玉 全 弄
木：本 末 机 杂 杯 果 板 相 桌 校 样 椅 楼 概 条 析 林 极 树 桔 架 柜 桥 集 橘
车：轻 较 辆
止：正 步 些 此
日：旧 早 时 明 易 春 是 星 昨 晚 晴 暖 音 旦 旱 晶
贝：贵 费 贺 货 贸
见：览 觉 视 观 现
牛：特 物
手：拿 拳 掰
欠：次 欢 歌 嗽 吹
殳：般 搬 没 锻
攵：收 改 教 散 数 敢 放
爪（爫）：爬 爱 采
斤：新 析 所 近
父：爸 爷
月：有 朋 服 脏 脱 期 明 青 肥 胖 胃 脸 脚 脑 能
方：放 旅 族 旗 房 旁
火：炼 烦 烧 灭 灾 灰 炎 灯
灬：点 热 然 照
户：房 扇
礻（示）：礼 视 祝 票
心：必 怎 您 想 感 意 思 念 忘 息 急 志 忽 愿

片:牌 版

五画

石:破 矿 码 岩 磁 碗

目:看 眼 睛 睡 盲

田:男 界 思 留 累 备 胃

钅:钱 铅 银 错 锻 铁 钟 钢

矢:知 短 矮

禾:和 利 种 香 秋 租 季

白:的 泉 皂

疒:病 瘦 疼 痛

立:亲 站 音 童

穴:穿 容 窗 空

衤:初 被 衬 衫 裙 裤 袜

疋:蛋 楚

鸟:鸡 鸭 鹅 鸣

皿:盘 盒

六画

耳:取 闻 职 聊

页:顾 预 题 颜 须 烦

虫:蛇 蚊 虾

竹:笔 第 等 答 算 篮 筷

舟:般 船 航

羽:扇 翻

羊(⺷):着 差 美

米:精 糖 料 粥

糸:系 累 紧

七画

走:起 越

酉:酒 酸 醉 醒

𧾷:跑 跟 路 踢

身:躺 躲

隹:难 集 准

八画

雨:雪 零 雷 需

九画

革:鞋

附录2

《汉字识写课本》主要部件构字表

匕:比 老 些 呢 嘴 能　　　　只:识 职

刀:切 分 初 绍 照 解　　　　生:星 醒 姓

力:历 办 加 务 边 助 动 男 努 驾　　示:票 漂 擦

又:友 观 双 汉 对 欢 鸡 努 取　　占:站 点 店

　　难 最　　　　　　　　　　　灬:蓝 篮 览

工:左 江 红 空 试 差 功 巧　　　冬:图 疼

寸:对 过 村 时 附 封 特 等 树　　可:哥 歌 河

　　射 谢　　　　　　　　　　　且:助 租 宜 谊 姐

大:因 美 套 椅 骑 奇 寄　　　　矢:医 知 矮 短 族

夂:备 处 冬 各 客 路 疼 图 条 务　乍:作 昨 怎

　　夏 复　　　　　　　　　　　令:零 铃 龄 冷 邻

亡:忙 忘　　　　　　　　　　　包:跑 饱 抱

己:记 起　　　　　　　　　　　乍:作 昨 怎

马:吗 妈 码　　　　　　　　　　包:饱 跑

子:字 好 学 游 孩 孙　　　　　加:架 驾 咖

井:讲 进　　　　　　　　　　　皮:破 被

中:种 钟　　　　　　　　　　　主:住 注 往

冈:刚 钢　　　　　　　　　　　立:位 拉 站 亲 童 音

化:花 货　　　　　　　　　　　圭:封 街 鞋

元:远 院 园 完 玩　　　　　　至:到 室 屋

云:层 运 动 会　　　　　　　　舌:刮 舍 话 活 适

耂:老 考 烤 教 都 猪　　　　　合:给 拿 盒 答

不:坏 还 杯　　　　　　　　　齐:挤 济

贝:贵 惯 赛 赢 贺 费 贸 货 员 圆　艮:跟 很 银 眼

牛:物 特 解　　　　　　　　　交:较 胶 校 郊 饺

斤:听 所 新 近 析　　　　　　亥:刻 咳 该 孩

反:版 板 饭　　　　　　　　　兑:说 阅 脱

勿:易 踢 物　　　　　　　　　甬:通 痛

殳:没 般 搬 锻　　　　　　　隹:难 谁 准 蕉 集

㕚:船 铅　　　　　　　　　　青:请 清 情 晴 精

方:放 房 访 旁 旅 族 旗 游　　京:凉 就 影

夬:快 块 筷 决　　　　　　　曷:喝 渴

巴:把 吧 爸 爬 肥 色　　　　禹:遇 寓

艮:服 报　　　　　　　　　　喿:操 澡

予:预 舒

附录 3

《汉字识写课本》声旁表音字表

声母、韵母、声调都相同

般——搬	中——钟
采——彩	坐——座
成——城	邦(bāng)——帮
旦——但	呈(chéng)——程
弟——第	董(dǒng)——懂
非——啡	段(duàn)——锻
哥——歌	朵(duǒ)——躲
工——功	番(fān)——翻
禾——和	付(fù)——附
合——盒	冈(gāng)——刚,钢
建——健	贯(guàn)——惯
介——界	胡(hú)——湖
库——裤	奂(huàn)——换
快——筷	及(jí)——级,极
力——历	焦(jiāo)——蕉
马——码	娄(lóu)——楼
冒——帽	曼(màn)——慢
其——旗	乃(nǎi)——奶
奇——骑	乔(qiáo)——桥
气——汽	求(qiú)——球
青——清	式(shì)——试
示——视	唐(táng)——糖
文——蚊	勿(wù)——物
元——园	永(yǒng)——泳
员——圆	由(yóu)——邮
止——址	占(zhàn)——站

声母、韵母相同,声调不同

巴——把,吧,爸	几——机
包——饱	己——记
采——菜	加——驾,架
长——张	交——较,饺
方——放,房,访	斤——近
化——花	两——辆

马——吗,妈	中——种
买——卖	主——住,注
门——们	子——字
那——哪	曷(hé)——喝
票——漂	韦(wéi)——伟
其——期	予(yǔ)——预
青——请,情	艮(gèn)——跟
人——认	召(zhāo)——照
下——虾	丙(bǐng)——病
相——想	昌(chāng)——唱
星——醒	官(guān)——馆
又——友	亡(wáng)——忘
羊——样	反(fǎn)——饭
宜——谊	奴(nú)——努
元——院,远	令(lìng)——零
原——愿	彦(yàn)——颜
比——毕	扁(biǎn)——遍
只——职	

声母同,韵母不同

见——觉	身——射
角——解	十——什
京——就	先——洗
井——进,讲	者——猪
两——俩	丁(dīng)——灯,打
录——绿	弗(fú)——费
母——每	吉(jí)——桔
你——您	令(lìng)——冷
化——货	尼(ní)——呢
少——沙	皮(pí)——破
舌——适,舍	央(yāng)——英
舍——舒	

声母不同,韵母相同

止——齿,此	包——跑
广——矿	方——旁
干——旱	奇——椅
齐——挤,济	早——草
青——精,睛	己——起
广——矿	至——室

易——踢
亲——新
京——影
完——院
矢——知,医
交——校
丁——厅
炎——谈
可——河
门——问,闻
元——完,玩
工——空,红
上——让
见——现
只——识
易——踢
苗(miáo)——猫
艮(gèn)——很
甲(jiǎ)——鸭

巴(ba)——爬
曷(hé)——渴
兹(zī)——磁
甬(yǒng)——通,痛
爰(yuán)——暖
尧(yáo)——烧
亡(wáng)——忙,盲
且(qiě)——姐
并(bìng)——瓶
尚(shàng)——常,躺,堂
乞(qǐ)——吃
君(jūn)——裙
勿(wù)——忽
叟(sǒu)——瘦
垂(chuí)——睡
反(fǎn)——版,板
司(sī)——词
召(zhāo)——绍

附录4

《汉字识写课本》生词索引

A

B

C

H

J

M

妈妈 māma　16

麻烦 máfan　18

马路 mǎlù　6

马马虎虎 mǎmǎ hūhū　6

马上 mǎshàng　6

买单 mǎidān　19

买东西 mǎi dōngxi　2

满意 mǎnyì　20

盲人 mángrén　24

毛笔 máobǐ　13

毛巾 máojīn　7

毛衣 máoyī　6

贸易 màoyì　17

帽子 màozi　17

没关系 méi guānxi　21

没什么 méi shénme　3

没意思 méi yìsi　15

没有 méiyǒu　3

每次 měi cì　18

每年 měi nián　14

每天 měi tiān　14

美好 měihǎo　24

美容 měiróng　24

美元 měiyuán　24

妹妹 mèimei　16

门口 ménkǒu　3

门票 ménpiào　13

梦见 mèngjiàn　16

面包 miànbāo　22

面条儿 miàntiáor　11

灭火 miè huǒ　24

民族 mínzú　18

名牌 míngpái　25

名片 míngpiàn　16

名字 míngzi　16

明白 míngbái　9

明年 míngnián　1

明天 míngtiān　1

鸣叫 míngjiào　23

墨水 mòshuǐ　24

母女 mǔnǚ　4

母亲 mǔqīn　10

木头 mùtou　5

目前 mùqián　4

N

哪儿 nǎr　9

哪个 nǎge　9

哪国人 nǎ guó rén　9

哪些 nǎxiē　11

那儿 nàr　3

那个 nàge　3

那么 nàme　3

那些 nàxiē　11

那样 nàyàng　11

奶奶 nǎinai　3

男孩 nánhái　10

男朋友 nán péngyou　24

男人 nánrén　24

南北 nánběi　3

南方 nánfāng　8

南京 Nánjīng　7

难过 nànguò　12

闹钟 nàozhōng　19

内容 nèiróng　24

你好 nǐ hǎo　2

你们 nǐmen　2

年级 niánjí　21

年轻 niánqīng　10

念课文 niàn kèwén　15

您好 nín hǎo　24

牛奶 niúnǎi　6

牛肉 niúròu　6

农民 nóngmín　8

农业 nóngyè　8

弄错 nòngcuò　24

弄清 nòngqīng　24

努力 nǔlì　18

女儿 nǚ'ér　4

女孩 nǚhái　10

女朋友 nǚ péngyou　24

女人 nǚrén　1

暖和 nuǎnhuo　9

P

爬山 pá shān　12

牌子 páizi　25

盘子 pánzi　19

旁边 pángbiān　22

胖子 pàngzi　16

跑步 pǎobù　11

朋友 péngyou　16

皮革 pígé　10

皮鞋 píxié　10

啤酒 píjiǔ　9

便宜 piányi　20

漂亮 piàoliang　20

Z

附录5

《汉字识写课本》生字索引

干 gān　8
敢 gǎn　22
感 gǎn　15
刚 gāng　15
钢 gāng　13
高 gāo　'7
告 gào　9
哥 gē　2
歌 gē　18
革 gé　10
个 gè　1
各 gè　22
给 gěi　25

跟 gēn　13
更 gēng　2
工 gōng　1
弓 gōng　19
公 gōng　3
功 gōng　10
共 gòng　1
狗 gǒu　21
顾 gù　17
瓜 guā　5
刮 guā　15
怪 guài　15

关 guān　1
观 guān　17
冠 guān　20
馆 guǎn　13
惯 guàn　15
光 guāng　24
广 guǎng　7
柜 guì　11
贵 guì　17
国 guó　24
果 guǒ　5
过 guò　21

H

孩 hái　10
海 hǎi　20
寒 hán　20
汉 hàn　1
旱 hàn　24
航 háng　16
好 hǎo　2
号 hào　9
喝 hē　9
禾 hé　12
合 hé　24
和 hé　12
河 hé　20
盒 hé　19

贺 hè　17
黑 hēi　24
很 hěn　3
红 hóng　21
后 hòu　2
候 hòu　14
忽 hū　15
湖 hú　20
虎 hǔ　6
互 hù　7
户 hù　18
花 huā　20
化 huà　14
划 huà　15

画 huà　19
话 huà　14
坏 huài　10
欢 huān　18
还 huán　21
换 huàn　15
黄 huáng　20
灰 huī　24
回 huí　6
会 huì　14
火 huǒ　5
或 huò　8
货 huò　17

J

机 jī　11
鸡 jī　19
级 jí　21
极 jí　11
急 jí　15
集 jí　11
几 jǐ　2
己 jǐ　8

挤 jǐ　15
记 jì　14
季 jì　12
济 jì　25
绩 jì　21
加 jiā　18
家 jiā　20
驾 jià　10

架 jià　11
假 jià　14
尖 jiān　24
间 jiān　19
见 jiàn　4
件 jiàn　14
建 jiàn　21
健 jiàn　14

M

妈 mā 16
麻 má 18
马 mǎ 6
码 mǎ 17
吗 ma 9
买 mǎi 2
卖 mài 8
满 mǎn 20
慢 màn 15
忙 máng 15
盲 máng 24
猫 māo 21
毛 máo 6

冒 mào 25
贸 mào 17
帽 mào 17
么 me 3
没 méi 3
每 měi 14
美 měi 24
妹 mèi 16
门 mén 3
们 men 3
梦 mèng 16
米 mǐ 5

面 miàn 4
灭 miè 24
民 mín 3
皿 mǐn 19
名 míng 16
明 míng 9
鸣 míng 23
末 mò 8
墨 mò 24
母 mǔ 4
木 mù 5
目 mù 4

N

拿 ná 15
哪 nǎ 9
那 nà 3
奶 nǎi 3
男 nán 24
南 nán 3
难 nán 12
脑 nǎo 16

闹 nào 19
呢 ne 9
能 néng 6
内 nèi 24
你 nǐ 2
年 nián 1
念 niàn 15
鸟 niǎo 6

您 nín 24
牛 niú 6
农 nóng 8
弄 nòng 24
努 nǔ 18
女 nǚ 1
暖 nuǎn 9

P

爬 pá 12
牌 pái 25
盘 pán 19
旁 páng 22
胖 pàng 16
跑 pǎo 13

朋 péng 16
啤 pí 9
匹 pǐ 22
片 piàn 8
漂 piāo 20
票 piào 13

品 pǐn 24
平 píng 25
苹 píng 20
瓶 píng 25
破 pò 17

Q

七 qī　2
妻 qī　16
期 qī　16
齐 qí　25
其 qí　19
骑 qí　10
旗 qí　18
起 qǐ　12
气 qì　5
汽 qì　23
千 qiān　1
铅 qiān　13

前 qián　3
钱 qián　13
欠 qiàn　18
桥 qiáo　11
巧 qiǎo　10
切 qiē　15
亲 qīn　10
青 qīng　16
轻 qīng　10
清 qīng　20
情 qíng　15
请 qǐng　14

庆 qìng　18
秋 qiū　12
球 qiú　10
区 qū　3
取 qǔ　23
去 qù　6
全 quán　14
泉 quán　17
拳 quán　15
犬 quǎn　21
裙 qún　13

R

然 rán　12
让 ràng　14
热 rè　12
人 rén　1

认 rèn　14
日 rì　5
容 róng　12

肉 ròu　6
如 rú　23
入 rù　8

S

赛 sài　20
三 sān　1
散 sàn　22
色 sè　15
森 sēn　24
沙 shā　23
山 shān　5
删 shān　23
衫 shān　13
扇 shàn　19
商 shāng　22
上 shàng　1
烧 shāo　12
勺 sháo　7
少 shào　1
绍 shào　25

舌 shé　4
蛇 shé　11
舍 shě　14
身 shēn　7
升 shēng　25
生 shēng　5
声 shēng　19
尸 shī　18
师 shī　17
十 shí　1
什 shí　14
石 shí　5
时 shí　16
识 shí　14
食 shí　6
矢 shǐ　12

使 shǐ　25
始 shǐ　23
士 shì　19
世 shì　25
市 shì　17
示 shì　13
事 shì　25
视 shì　17
试 shì　14
室 shì　24
是 shì　9
适 shì　25
收 shōu　22
手 shǒu　4
首 shǒu　4
瘦 shòu　21

鲜 xiān 23　　　些 xiē 11　　　行 xíng 6
现 xiàn 10　　　鞋 xié 10　　　醒 xǐng 19
相 xiāng 11　　　写 xiě 20　　　姓 xìng 16
香 xiāng 12　　　谢 xiè 14　　　休 xiū 14
想 xiǎng 15　　　心 xīn 2　　　须 xū 22
向 xiàng 7　　　新 xīn 17　　　需 xū 25
象 xiàng 6　　　信 xìn 23　　　学 xué 2
小 xiǎo 4　　　兴 xīng 1　　　雪 xuě 16
校 xiào 11　　　星 xīng 9　　　血 xuè 8

Y

鸭 yā 19　　　以 yǐ 3　　　又 yòu 4
牙 yá 4　　　椅 yǐ 11　　　右 yòu 22
延 yán 21　　　译 yì 14　　　鱼 yú 6
言 yán 14　　　易 yì 9　　　羽 yǔ 6
岩 yán 24　　　谊 yì 25　　　雨 yǔ 5
炎 yán 24　　　意 yì 15　　　语 yǔ 3
颜 yán 17　　　因 yīn 22　　　玉 yù 7
眼 yǎn 9　　　阴 yīn 23　　　预 yù 17
演 yǎn 20　　　音 yīn 9　　　寓 yù 25
羊 yáng 6　　　银 yín 13　　　遇 yù 21
阳 yáng 23　　　饮 yǐn 13　　　元 yuán 2
样 yàng 11　　　应 yīng 18　　　员 yuán 17
要 yào 16　　　英 yīng 20　　　园 yuán 22
爷 yé 16　　　迎 yíng 21　　　原 yuán 18
也 yě 3　　　影 yǐng 22　　　圆 yuán 22
业 yè 1　　　泳 yǒng 20　　　远 yuǎn 21
页 yè 17　　　用 yòng 8　　　院 yuàn 21
一 yī 1　　　邮 yóu 21　　　愿 yuàn 15
衣 yī 7　　　游 yóu 20　　　月 yuè 5
医 yī 22　　　友 yǒu 24　　　阅 yuè 19
宜 yí 20　　　有 yǒu 3　　　越 yuè 12
已 yǐ 8　　　酉 yǒu 19　　　云 yún 5

Z

杂 zá 11　　　在 zài 10　　　澡 zǎo 20
灾 zāi 24　　　脏 zāng 16　　　皂 zào 17
再 zài 3　　　早 zǎo 9　　　怎 zěn 15